“Trauma affects everyone, and yet as B

care is not for the faint-hearted and is

overworked. *From Burned Out to Beloved* takes us on an important journey of self-discovery, enabling us to balance contemplation and activism in a way that brings healing and wholeness. This is an important book for all who feel the growing pressures of ministry.”

Christine Sine, author of *The Gift of Wonder: Creative Practices for Delighting in God*

“*From Burned Out to Beloved* literally woos us as service providers and as leaders to slow down, to breathe in deeply the knowledge we are the Trinity’s beloved child, and to be transformed! For twenty-two years I was the executive director of New Horizons, a ministry for homeless youth and young women involved in prostitution. Those years taught me and those I served with much about the trauma that can come into one’s soul as we loved and served those in great need. We learned—through listening to the Trinity, practicing vulnerability with each other, and many trials and errors—much of the truth Bethany profoundly shares through her book. She has encapsulated significant truth, depth of understanding, and tools to embrace spiritual, emotional, and physical wholeness while learning from those you serve. For the last twelve years I have served as a spiritual director to Christian leaders and have seen the vital truths Bethany teaches us transform the lives of leaders who are weary and in need. I deeply encourage you to read this book slowly, to engage in Bethany’s suggested practices, and to learn the joy of burning without being consumed. Just as Scripture calls out, this is holy ground.”

Rita Nussli, spiritual director with SoulFormation

“What Bethany Dearborn Hiser offers here is essential for every pastor, social worker, caregiver, or friend: a gaze into the groaning beauty of being human. Her vision of this mystery is candid, sustained, tender, and hopeful. Holistic life and ministry has seldom been portrayed as more inspiring, or as more daunting. Hiser gives those of us in ministry a clear reminder that human beings reflect the exquisite glory of God’s design as well as our human proclivity to be victims and perpetrators of our own worst instincts. Therein lies the glory and agony of the human journey that every teenager, young adult, client, older parishioner, family, or small group must face. Our individual and collective need for credible hope turns first on God’s gift in Jesus Christ and also on our readiness to live nothing more, but nothing less, than a truly human life—for our sake and our neighbor’s. This is the mission of God’s grace in every ministry setting. I’m grateful that Hiser helps us see why we need this ourselves and how to live it in freedom and joy, more than in exhaustion.”

Mark Labberton, president of Fuller Theological Seminary

"*From Burned Out to Beloved* is an essential roadmap for those who want to be of service. We welcome our wounds and shift how we see. We don't go to the margins to make a difference but to be made different by those we encounter there. Hiser's book leads the way."

Father Greg Boyle, founder of Homeboy Industries

"Bethany Dearborn Hiser offers the reader a refreshingly bold and practical resource for those seeking healthier patterns toward wholeness and sustainability. Grounded in her experience and research, Hiser is not afraid to name critical intersections of race and gender and how those identities inform one's lens of engagement in the world. This book is a must-read for those who think they already have it figured out!"

Gail Song Bantum, lead pastor of Quest Church, Seattle

"If you are picking up this book, you probably have a huge heart for the desperate and broken ones on the earth. This is beautiful, but if you try to save the world in your own strength, you will be extremely burned out. Bethany Dearborn Hiser could attest to that. Then God led her on a journey of recovery and reflection, and this powerful book was birthed through the process. During our first years in Mozambique rescuing abandoned children from the streets and praying for daily provision, I also reached my limits. I just wanted to go work at K-Mart, but then God encountered me in a radical way. He taught me to abide in him. John 14 and 15 became my life verses. As you read these pages, let God do a deep work in your heart and lead you into his fullness. God wants to encounter you and fill you with the oil of his presence. He wants to reshape your ideas about who you are and how you're called to minister. We are the lovers of Jesus, the body of Christ. We are fully accepted in him. Living from the secret place, we can truly burn for him and not burn out!"

Heidi G. Baker, cofounder and executive chairman of the board, Iris Global

"*From Burned Out to Beloved* is a tremendous resource for Christians involved in the caring vocations. Bethany has shared her own honest and raw story of burnout as well as recovery, and the lifelong journey that entails. As she states, 'Our theology, trauma exposure, and shame can all impact our behavior and beliefs.' Bethany makes good connections between Scripture and the beliefs that impact Christians in the helping professions, while guiding readers to excellent resources, reflective questions, and spiritual practices to heal the soul and help maintain caregiver health."

Michelle O'Rourke, consultant with the Henri Nouwen Society, author of *Healthy Caregiving*

"Bethany Dearborn Hiser used 'invincible' to describe herself during her early years of doing social work. I have known Bethany for many years, and I can testify that she did seem invincible. But as she relates, her invincibility came crashing down. This wonderful book tells the story of how wrong she was, and how wrong all of us are when we serve as if we were God's equal. Facing classic burnout, she discovered what it means to live in grace and freedom, to know one is beloved, to learn to rest and play, all the while continuing to serve. This book is a banquet of insight, beauty, truth, and practical wisdom. I started to read it to honor Bethany's request for an endorsement. It did not take me long to discover how much I needed to read it for me. Thank you, Bethany, for this helpful, honest, elegant little book!"

Gerald L. Sittser, professor of theology at Whitworth University, author of *A Grace Disguised*

"Bethany Dearborn Hiser's *From Burned Out to Beloved* is a great resource for all who have found themselves on the verge of being burned out doing service and wondering where God is. Her honest retelling of her story makes this book more a companion than a condemning voice, as she invites the reader to experience becoming the beloved of God. Hiser integrates psychological and theological resources to provide a deeper understanding of how to serve others and thrive, both thoughtfully and practically. The question is not, How do we serve, but from what sources do we draw to do service? For those of us who train people to think of communal service as a lifestyle, this is an important lesson in teaching them how to flourish."

J. Derek McNeil, president and provost, the Seattle School of Theology and Psychology

"Applicable. Accessible. Essential. *From Burned Out to Beloved* gently and authentically challenges false belief systems, especially for those of us addicted to helping, overcommitting, and saying yes. Bethany Dearborn Hiser addresses the barriers that keep us from living fully from our true selves and provides applicable guidance toward healing and freedom. The text is vivid with concrete stories and examples, full of practical steps and guides, and grounded in prayer and authentic connection with God. Hiser looks not just at the why of burnout but even deeper at the motives behind our work . . . and at the how of healing, with clear steps toward freedom and growth. The text sings of God's deep love for us and our ultimate need for connection with him to sustain any meaningful work we do. This is a relevant and critical guide for anyone who is involved in ministry and people-centered work. We're adopting it as part of our staff-training program as an essential read."

Hannah Bryant, executive director of Leadership Mission International

"A former detective of child molestation and murder cases once told me, 'Detectives in this field don't last long. They either quit or burn out after a few years.' I've seen the same thing happen to those living and serving in marginalized communities. If Jesus calls us to insert ourselves into the wounds of society as agents of healing, how are we to keep from becoming swallowed up by those wounds? Bethany Dearborn Hiser has discovered the pathway out of secondary trauma and burnout. She found that walking alongside those experiencing domestic abuse, incarceration, and drug addiction was a gift, waking her to her own brokenness, poverty, and limitations. But it was also a slippery slope into a messianic complex and codependency. *From Burned Out to Beloved* is the personal protective equipment required for those serving in a global pandemic of violence and sorrow."

Scott Bessenecker, director of global engagement and Justice, InterVarsity Christian Fellowship/USA

FROM

BURNED OUT

TO

BELOVED

SOUL CARE FOR WOUNDED HEALERS

BETHANY DEARBORN HISER

An imprint of InterVarsity Press
Downers Grove, Illinois

InterVarsity Press
P.O. Box 1400, Downers Grove, IL 60515-1426
ivpress.com
email@ivpress.com

InterVarsity Press® is the book-publishing division of InterVarsity Christian Fellowship/USA®, a movement of students and faculty active on campus at hundreds of universities, colleges, and schools of nursing in the United States of America, and a member movement of the International Fellowship of Evangelical Students. For information about local and regional activities, visit intervarsity.org.

While all stories in this book are true, some names and identifying information may have been changed to protect the privacy of individuals.

Cover design and image composite: Faceout Studio
Interior design: Daniel van Loon

ISBN 978-0-8308-4795-2 (print)
ISBN 978-0-8308-4796-9 (digital)

Printed in the United States of America ♾

InterVarsity Press is committed to ecological stewardship and to the conservation of natural resources in all our operations. This book was printed using sustainably sourced paper.

Library of Congress Cataloging-in-Publication Data
A catalog record for this book is available from the Library of Congress.

P 21 20 19 18 17 16 15 14 13 12 11 10 9 8 7 6 5 4 3 2 1
Y 36 35 34 33 32 31 30 29 28 27 26 25 24 23 22 21 20

TO MY BELOVED KENNY

Because of you, this book exists.
Because of you, I am more grounded in my
identity as a beloved one.

CONTENTS

Introduction: Confessions of a Social Justice Workaholic *1*

PART ONE: CENTERING

1 Trauma-Informed Soul Care *11*

2 Living As Beloved *27*

3 Wounded Healers *37*

PART TWO: UNPACKING

4 Secondary Trauma *47*

5 Codependency in the Workplace *56*

6 Needs and Desires *67*

7 False Beliefs *77*

PART THREE: RECOVERING

8 Identifying Stages of Change *87*

9 Moving from Shame to Self-Empathy *98*

10 Embracing Our Need for Others *108*

11 Changing Beliefs and Behaviors *116*

PART FOUR: THRIVING

12 Discerning When to Say No and When to Say Yes *131*

13 Creating Rhythms of Rest and Renewal *141*

14 Living in Joy *159*

Conclusion *170*

Acknowledgments *175*

Appendix One: Grounding Practices *178*

Appendix Two: Reflections and Prayer Exercises *181*

Notes *188*

INTRODUCTION

Confessions of a Social Justice Workaholic

I used to think self-care was trivial. It was a luxury I didn't need or deserve. I spent my days working with people facing homelessness, abuse, addiction, and incarceration. I felt guilty taking time for myself in the face of so much injustice and poverty and thought my passion for the work would carry me through.

I'm not sure exactly when my burnout started. When I look back at journal writings from even the early days of my social-work career, I see signs of despair, exhaustion, misplaced guilt, and inadequacy.

About five years before I burned out, I was working for the first time as a case manager at one of the largest service providers for people experiencing homelessness in downtown Seattle. It was my role to assist the "employable homeless" in finding housing and employment. Although I had previously volunteered as a mentor in juvenile detention, organized youth service trips in Seattle, and lived and studied in Central America, I was in over my head. I wrote in my journal: "I am completely overwhelmed right now. Socked in the stomach, overcome by grief, infuriated at the injustice and disparity that exists in the world—the absolutely insane violation of people's basic human rights. I feel like I'm not really moving anything forward. It's not enough. When will it ever be enough?"

One of my clients, Simon, struggled with depression, alcoholism, diabetes, and suicidal thoughts. Every week I urged him to stay in a shelter. He never did. I didn't blame him. I wouldn't want to sleep in a shelter either. Many shelters in the city were large dorm rooms with twenty-five or more bunkbeds. They were noisy, often chaotic, and sometimes unsafe. Clients had to leave early in the morning and wait in line each night to get in. The lack of privacy and unpredictability alone was dehumanizing and stressful.

Often on cold and rainy evenings, I bused home through the International District, imagining Simon heading to his tent in the rain or snow. His particular struggles weighed on me. I remember arriving home and staring out at the downpour, grieved and worried for Simon's well-being, and struck by my inability to do anything to change his situation.

Not long into the job, I started a master's degree in social work. I already knew I was struggling to handle the work, but I thought I just needed more training. For three years, I studied while working two part-time case-management jobs. I simultaneously took classes, researched sex trafficking, managed a drop-in center for migrant farmworkers, and accompanied families as they faced deportation, abuse, and the everyday grind of barely making ends meet. Twice a week, I led domestic-violence support groups and staffed the women's shelter until midnight. I organized a coalition to address local sex trafficking and held monthly meetings for law enforcement professionals, social workers, community leaders, and educators.

There was always more to do. I rarely slowed down, let alone considered vacations. My family spent a week at a nearby cabin each summer, and instead of joining them, I drove down just for an afternoon or maybe an overnight. Then I went back to work. When I took time off, it was to visit organizations working with former sex workers in Thailand and Cambodia.

I didn't give myself permission to play or to do anything solely for fun or relaxation. I only read novels and watched movies that had a globally significant storyline.

I felt that I didn't deserve or couldn't afford to take care of myself in the face of so much suffering. Saying no felt like either a liability or an expression of disdain for the needs of others and for myself.

When I recognized my exhaustion and compassion fatigue, I judged myself. I thought, *Who am I to complain? My life is full of blessings that go far beyond my essential needs.*

I heard countless stories of trauma directly from survivors as well as time after time from my community. I had very few boundaries and answered calls at all hours. More than once I agreed to go to the hospital for sexual assault calls because I happened to live closer than other staff. I could take it for the team. I thought I was invincible.

My mind began to feel saturated with traumatic realities. Pressing on felt easier than making changes. I also didn't want to stop engaging and advocating for changes. I felt called to the work and grateful for the gift of listening and knowing people's stories. I wanted to move forward, to move mountains of societal barriers.

Over time my obsession with always doing the work had chipped away at my ability to do the work at all. I didn't yet realize the impact of my internal narratives and belief systems.

Slowly my identity became more and more centered on what I did, rather than who I was. I started to believe that my identity and worth were based on helping others. Worse, I thought I didn't have value as a person unless I was serving people in need. I couldn't stop doing this type of work, because I was called, because I cared, because I was addicted. Beneath my compassion was a drive—even a need for meaning and self-worth.

TIME TO TURN AROUND

During the final year of my master's degree, a fellow student encouraged me to take a class called "Self-Care for Social Workers." I resisted. It sounded tedious. They would probably just tell me I needed to exercise, eat healthy food, rest, and write a self-care plan. I didn't think I needed it. I thought I was already doing those things—and I had too much to do in general.

Despite my doubts—and with some persuasion—I signed up for the class. The two eight-hour sessions taught by Laura van Dernoot Lipsky helped catalyze my new journey. The course and her book *Trauma Stewardship* opened my eyes to the impact my work was having on me and helped me to see that I desperately needed help.

I began to learn that trauma affects everyone who is exposed to it. This includes not only those plagued by violence, homelessness, and addiction, but also the social workers, therapists, pastors, relief workers, and community development workers who try to help. Psychologists call this secondary trauma or vicarious trauma. It is the trauma that comes with repeatedly hearing the stories of and working with people in crisis. In the same way firefighters can be stained with soot and ash, I was covered with the residue of my own work.

Secondary trauma is normal and hard to avoid, so I didn't need to apologize for being affected or for needing help.

Learning how affected I was by trauma was one thing. Yet making changes and moving forward was another. I realized I needed to be saved, but not from the difficulty of the work. I needed to be saved from my unhealthy motives and beliefs that had led me to dark spaces.

Before I experienced burnout, I thought self-care was superficial. In popular culture, *self-care* often means nothing more than pampering. Social media is littered with posts that equate self-care with massages and manicures. *I'm in need of some good self-care! Looking for recommendations for a great massage, nail salon, and eyebrow wax!* Many think they can't afford or they don't deserve this kind of self-care.

As I've worked through my own barriers to self-care, I've come to see that taking care of myself involves deeper inner healing and recovery as well as more integrated practices than occasional excursions to the salon. For me, it is about connection to God, who not only sustains and partners with me but also helps me to accept my brokenness and tend to my wounds. It involves knowing that I am beloved, regardless of what I do.

Now I confess that I am in recovery of being a social-justice messiah-complex workaholic.

And I'm not alone. I know many who are also desperate for support, burning out, and leaving their work. They're longing to be resilient as they live out their calling and yearning to know the God of love who accepts and supports them as they are. Instead of feeling invigorated by their work, they are discouraged, depleted, and depressed. Perhaps you are one of them.

WELCOME TO THE JOURNEY

I don't intend to offer you a detailed explanation of how we are affected by the work or by trauma in general. Many excellent resources have been published on self-care, resilience, compassion fatigue, trauma exposure, and burnout. If you're experiencing PTSD-like symptoms such as flashbacks and triggers, know that this book is not a substitute for professional help. I encourage you to pursue therapy and resources such as John Henden's *What It Takes to Thrive: Techniques for Severe Trauma and Stress Recovery.*

I invite you to join me on a journey that weaves together trauma research, spiritual practices, addiction recovery, and inner healing. Although I've gained much from others' perspectives, my offerings largely stem from walking through the fire of my own burnout.

I don't pretend you are driven by the same struggles or beliefs I have. I'm a white American woman with a master's degree. I acknowledge that my social location and family history impact my paradigm and include explicit and implicit privileges. There are many forms of secondary as well as primary trauma that I've never had to endure. While I hope to share my journey in a way that connects with you, I know that my perspective is limited. I'm still learning, and sometimes I may miss the mark. By God's grace, I hope that, with this book, you know your beloved self more deeply, establish life-giving rhythms, and are further equipped in recovery from secondary trauma, workaholism, and codependency.

I believe that together we can journey toward basing our identity on being God's beloveds instead of on what we do or what others say about us. We can walk together toward freedom and grace instead of in desperation to make a difference. We can learn to love ourselves as we love our neighbors. This is a journey of pride and brokenness, of learning to say no and to ask for help. It's a journey of forgiveness and healing that involves learning to combine contemplation with activism and being with doing.

This work is worth it, because you are worth it. It's also worth it because, as you heal, you'll become more resilient. Your work will be more sustainable and effective, and you will have the tools and insight to enhance the structures and systems you are a part of, fostering environments that encourage others to live sustainably as well.

Soul care is not for the faint of heart. Yet, to thrive—let alone survive—in this work, soul care is not optional. It is essential.

WHAT WE WILL FIND

We will first look at the importance of living out of our identity as beloved children of God and of welcoming our woundedness. In part two, we'll look at some barriers to caring for ourselves: the effects of secondary trauma, codependency, unmet needs, and personal beliefs. In part three, we'll delve into ways of pursuing recovery. In part four, we'll focus on learning to thrive in our work.

Each chapter includes exercises to choose from in order to take small steps toward change. In the appendices you'll find grounding practices and listening prayer exercises to aid in your work of recovery and healing.

I'm grateful you've chosen to join me on the journey. To bless you on the way, here is a poem by Jan Richardson, "A Blessing for Traveling in the Dark."

> Go slow
> if you can.
> Slower.
> More slowly still.
> Friendly dark
> or fearsome,
> this is no place
> to break your neck
> by rushing,
> by running,
> by crashing into
> what you cannot see.
> Then again,
> it is true:
> different darks
> have different tasks,

and if you
have arrived here unawares,
if you have come
in peril
or in pain,
this might be no place
you should dawdle.
I do not know
what these shadows
ask of you,
what they might hold
that means you good
or ill.
It is not for me
to reckon
whether you should linger
or you should leave.
But this is what
I can ask for you:
That in the darkness
there be a blessing.
That in the shadows
there be a welcome.
That in the night
you be encompassed
by the Love that knows
your name.

PART ONE

CENTERING

We are perfectly loved with a love that requires nothing of us, so we can stop "being good" and live into the goodness that is our essence. . . . God holds out an invitation to us—an invitation to turn away from the anxious striving that has turned stress into a status symbol. It is an invitation to wholeness that leads to flourishing for all of us.

ARCHBISHOP DESMOND TUTU AND MPHO TUTU

ONE

TRAUMA-INFORMED SOUL CARE

Sometimes resilience arrives in the moment you discover your own unshakeable goodness. . . . And when that happens, we begin to foster tenderness for our own human predicament. A spacious and undefended heart finds room for everything you are and carves space for everybody else.

FATHER GREG BOYLE, *TATTOOS ON THE HEART*

Prior to burnout, I was working two part-time advocacy jobs that added up to much more than full-time. One of the jobs was with Tierra Nueva, an international Christian ministry based in Burlington, Washington, that loves and accompanies people who are primarily affected by addiction, incarceration, and immigration. The other was at a domestic violence shelter, providing advocacy and support for survivors of domestic violence and sexual assault. Throughout most of my days, I sought to listen empathetically to people's stories while suppressing my shock and grief at what they shared. Sometimes I let tears show, yet I fought hard to hold my emotions at bay and receive their stories with compassion.

A significant turning point came during a domestic violence advocacy appointment with a primarily Spanish-speaking mother. I was in the midst of translating a letter written by her daughter, who had been detained by immigration. For the first time, the daughter was revealing that she'd been in an abusive relationship for years. She described details of the abuse and revealed the shame that had driven her to keep it a secret.

Her mother's grief was palpable, yet through her tears, she asked me to continue reading. I read as my own tears started to fall. Suddenly the mother cried out, "Por qué los hombres hacen eso?" ("Why do men do this?") It was a question I myself had been grappling with, and the floodgates opened. We both sobbed and sobbed.

This moment broke something open in me. I lost my ability to listen empathetically and keep my emotions in control. My professional social-work armor of showing care but not being vulnerable had disintegrated. All the unprocessed stories had been piling up in me. I sobbed not just for this mother and her daughter but also for the many who had experienced similar abuse; all those stories I still carried with me. While tears can sometimes be connecting, I wasn't able to be present with that mother as my own grief poured out.

I left that meeting knowing I needed to make some changes. I couldn't stem the tide of tears. I took an emergency week off not long after that—to address my own mental health. I felt like I couldn't function. The grief, stress, lack of boundaries, and accumulated secondary trauma overwhelmed me. I was exhausted physically, emotionally, and mentally.

Desperate for respite, I drove to my parents' cabin, barely able to see through the tears that flowed. My armor had cracked, and I didn't know how to handle it.

Without realizing it, I was experiencing textbook burnout. I was overcome by emotional exhaustion, which is at the heart of the "burnout syndrome," according to Christine Maslach, author of *Burnout: The Cost of Caring*. "A person gets overly involved emotionally, overextends him- or herself, and feels overwhelmed by the demands imposed by other people. . . . Once emotional exhaustion sets in, people feel they are no longer able to give of themselves to others." The second burnout symptom is depersonalization, or a "detached, callous and even dehumanized response." I didn't want to get to that point of detachment and was grateful I was still able to grieve. Yet I knew I needed to make some changes for my own well-being and to avoid becoming unable to care well for the person in front of me.

Although it took years to feel healthier and more grounded, I began to make some initial adjustments. I quit my job at the domestic violence shelter and moved farther away from the hospital and the center of town to create better boundaries with Tierra Nueva's pastoral advocacy work. In this newfound space and time, I delved into inner-healing prayer appointments, therapy, and recovery work. I also slowly started integrating new rhythms of rest.

BURNOUT AS ALTITUDE SICKNESS

In some ways, burnout can be compared to altitude sickness. A few years ago, my husband and I hiked the Annapurna Trail in the Himalayas. This gorgeous trail starts in a tropical jungle at a low elevation and climbs to a 17,769-foot mountain pass. For many, that might not be appealing, but I was thrilled to be on that hike before heading to Kolkata, India. Aware of the immense privilege, I was aiming to live into my newfound permission to enjoy fun adventures.

Halfway into the trek, I was struggling with a bad cough and diarrhea. After crossing a one-hundred-foot narrow suspension footbridge over a deep ravine at ten thousand feet in elevation, I sat down on a large rock and passed out. I had never passed out before. My terrified husband yelled for help to hikers behind us. Not understanding English, they were about to pass by when they saw a look of desperation on his face.

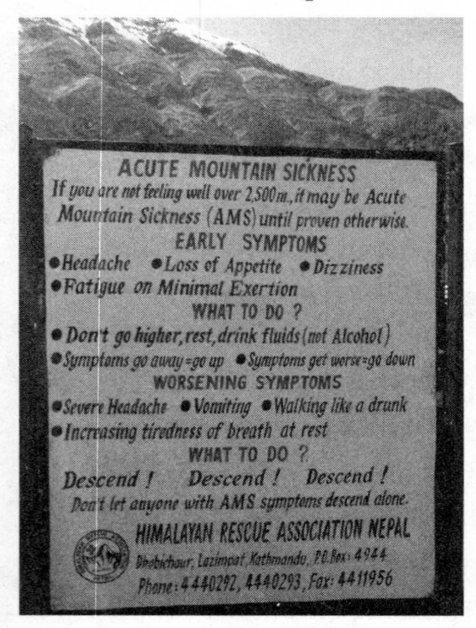

I woke up surrounded by my husband and a group of Italians. After resting and drinking some water, we retraced our steps back down the mountain, knowing that the remedy for altitude sickness is to go downward.

As this photo of a poster in the Himalayas says, "Descend! Descend! Descend!" Quite literally, if you don't go down to a lower elevation, you will die.

Ironically, people who are physically fit are more susceptible to altitude sickness. They ascend faster than their bodies can adjust to the higher altitude. They press on, thinking they're capable, and they don't listen to their bodies' cues. While hiking, I had been denying what my body had been communicating to me for days—that I needed to rest and recover. In the same way, we can mistakenly think that we are "above burnout," that we're strong enough and don't need care. But those beliefs make us more susceptible to burning out. We press on, disregarding the need for rest that our body might be communicating through headaches, stomachaches, fatigue, and an inability to think clearly or creatively. We keep going until an emergency hits, and we're forced to take a break.

Attaining rest can be especially challenging, even if we're able to change our circumstances or quit our job. Immigrant rights advocate Sayu Bhojwani describes how people of color feel overwhelmed "not just about resources, but also about feeling like we don't have the time or the luxury to take a break. We feel guilty caring for ourselves, or even for a child or loved one." She continues, "Denial of our authentic selves, coupled with the scarcity mentality and a competitive culture, wears us down." Exposure to continuous racism and institutionalized oppression can cause people of color to develop post-traumatic stress syndromes. Housing insecurity, illness, family issues, and gender discrimination may also compound workplace trauma. It's understandable to feel overwhelmed by the weight of the work and surrounding realities.

Other organizational pressures and unhealthy workplace dynamics also increase the likelihood of burnout. In America's white-dominated environments, it's all too common for exhaustion to be a barometer for success. Busier is better. I've felt ashamed for being at home sleeping instead of out at midnight like my colleague, who drove to visit young women sitting beside their gunshot boyfriends at the trauma center. Instead of honoring one another's hard work and welcoming our limitations, we act as though tiredness is proof that we're loving and caring for people well.

Many face a high level of need and an intense client/student/patient caseload with little support and heavy paperwork requirements. Some teachers buy breakfast for students because schools and parents can't provide it. Social workers often manage extra-large caseloads because of lack of funding. Societal systems of injustice and oppression feel out of our control. We're weighed down and aggrieved by the hunger, abuse, neglect, and mental illness that we witness.

Many have had to learn how to breathe at toxic altitudes. The ability to descend can be especially difficult, and thriving—let alone surviving—depends on finding ways to do so, even though trauma takes its toll.

Social workers, church leaders, ministry workers, therapists, foster parents, medical professionals, and teachers are often passionately serving our communities, yet all too often we are burning out and leaving the work. As noted in a 2018 Leadership Resources article, "[Fifteen hundred] pastors leave the ministry each month due to moral failure, spiritual burnout, or contention in their churches."

What if instead of busyness being the barometer, we encouraged one another to work with greater self-awareness and to live grounded and at peace?

What if we acknowledged our wounds instead of pretending they don't affect us?

What if we reckoned with how we have experienced oppression or privilege and with how that has diminished our view of ourselves and others?

What if we honestly engaged with the internal beliefs and values that distort our self-perception and gave ourselves permission to thrive?

What if we served out of a deep certainty that we—and all people—are beloved, just as we are, regardless of how we change or help others to change?

Just as with altitude sickness, the remedy for burnout is to go down and rest. Although physical changes may be required, the descent is largely into our own depths, where we explore our barriers and connect with the deep well of God's presence within us.

FROM SELF-CARE TO SOUL CARE

Many social workers would say that self-care is important, but in practice we feel that it's one more thing to do with no time to do it. Institutional encouragement to practice self-care is often ineffective without the social worker having an understanding of secondary trauma and other internal barriers.

I've created numerous self-care plans at various workshops. Usually they involve looking at what the participants lack and creating plans to change that. For example, at one group session, I was invited to look at my life as a circle, with various areas that need tending to, such as physical, emotional, psychological, spiritual, and relational. We colored in each pie wedge to the degree we felt fulfilled in that area. Next we described what activities we needed to do to fill each piece up.

At a training for clergy and spiritual teachers on healthy boundaries, we used the Self-Care Inventory, which ranged from "I play a musical instrument and practice regularly" to "I eat most evening meals with my partner/family." Not only were these exercises based on privilege, but as I looked at my blank inventory and empty pie wedges, they also left me feeling inadequate and exhausted. How could I possibly find the time or energy to do what it would take to fill up all those areas? Where would I find the resources? Although such reflection has sometimes been helpful, more often than not I've felt unmotivated to change—or changing felt too hard and out of reach. Deeper soul care is needed to establish our identity as beloved, to explore the beliefs that drive our unhealthy behaviors, and to equip us to take care of ourselves.

The practice of holistic, trauma-informed soul care tends to the whole self in order to be grounded in God, to thrive, and to love others as we love ourselves. It involves knowing *who* we are, *how* we're impacted by secondary trauma, and *why* we must be on an ongoing journey toward recovery and healing.

Taking care of ourselves is essential for our well-being as beloved children of God, allowing us to be effective and resilient, loving people instead of using those we serve to support or enhance our own sense of worth. Here are the central soul care ideas we'll explore throughout this book.

We are beloved children of God. God loves us not for what we do or don't do. We can't do anything to make God love us more or less. We are deeply loved. Living out of our belovedness involves learning to receive love and to extend care to ourselves. We're invited to know ourselves, our motivations for our work, our desires, and the ways our unmet needs play out in how we engage the world.

Our inner beliefs and perceptions affect our care for others and ourselves. The beliefs we hold about ourselves can drive us to burnout. Without our awareness, false beliefs drive our feelings of anger, shame, guilt, or unworthiness. We end up less able to care for the person in front of us and more likely to be depleted due to stress and lack of rest. When such patterns continue, they often lead to utter exhaustion and even symptoms of post-traumatic stress. Some feel so disillusioned and disheartened that they leave their work or ministry—and even their faith. Understanding our beliefs is an important step to free us from shame and to help us move toward wholeness and resilience.

As we work with people in the midst of trauma, taking care of ourselves is not optional; it is essential. Soul care is for all people, not just those who feel weak or who are spiritually oriented. Secondary trauma—the emotional and physiological toll of hearing about another person's first-hand experience of trauma—is a well-documented phenomenon that can affect anyone. It's compounded when we carry our own personal trauma as well. Understanding its effect can increase our compassion for ourselves, our awareness of how we are being impacted, and our motivation to discover sustainable practices.

Being rooted in God and practicing holistic soul care benefits us as well as those around us. Self-care that engages spiritual practices has been shown to prevent burnout and improve coping strategies. When we partner with God, honor healthy boundaries, and commit to rhythms of rest, we are freer and healthier in our love and care for people. We live, move, and breathe knowing we are held securely in God's love, and we are able to love others out of a place of fullness rather than emptiness and striving. We tap into God's abundance and feel inspired by our work. We know we are worthy of care ourselves, regardless of what impact we have.

EMBRACING INNER WORK

Although I knew I needed to rest, to re-center in God, and to create better boundaries, I wasn't able to slow down. The real and perceived needs around me determined my pace. I had become addicted to busyness, and enjoyed the adrenaline boost that helping people in crisis brought. It was hard to give myself margins of rest and play. Often I stopped by someone's house on the way home, squeezing in one last visit. This meant I would be late to my next appointment or dinner with friends. When I got home, I kept going: paying bills, responding to emails, and even doing non-urgent things, such as planning an event.

> *To live the questions requires that you first look within yourself, trusting that God is present and at work within you.*
> HENRI NOUWEN

Juggling jobs, maintaining a household, and paying bills is often necessary to keep afloat. However, this is different from keeping busy to avoid processing or feeling emotions. I can now see how my pace of life was part of my coping strategy. I believed I needed to be productive. I didn't allow myself to stop.

Soul care requires that we slow down, because our pace of life likely prevents us from asking questions and facing traumatic realities. Poet David Whyte wrote, "Not only can we become afraid of these internal questions, but also we can become terrified of the spaces or silences in which these questions might arise. The act of stopping can be the act of facing something we have kept hidden from ourselves for a very long time." When we start asking questions, we begin dismantling our false self. (We'll explore this more throughout.) Whyte also wrote, "There is no first step toward self-knowledge without hazard or risk to the surface self you already know."

In the same way that the soul is nonmaterial and unseen, as psychologist David Benner illuminates, so are the barriers to taking care of ourselves. If we just make goals and don't address the internal barriers and the ways we are affected by trauma, our self-care plan will be just another thing we feel we aren't doing well.

Taking an emergency week off was the "descent" that prevented further calamity in my life. I hadn't recognized my own brokenness and inability to take care of myself. I had been ignoring my physical and emotional exhaustion. A kind of rescue came to me through a relapse-prevention program called the Genesis Process, where I started recognizing my subtle and not-so-subtle unhealthy patterns. Experiencing care for my own soul opened my eyes to the need to live beyond my understanding of self-care into something that tended to my *soul*.

At first I thought the changes I made post-burnout were sufficient. When I told a respected pastor a bit about my burnout story and my need for an emergency week off, his reply shocked me: "Only a week?! I was laid flat for a year after burning out."

I was amazed; I couldn't imagine taking that much time off. Yet after a couple of years of working while implementing my newfound practices, I still wasn't healthy. I realized I too needed more time to heal and to figure out how to make my work sustainable before I did greater damage. I was gifted with the freedom to take a sabbatical so I could rest, heal, and consider what was next.

Doing inner work is never easy. We prefer quick solutions and easy answers. Who wouldn't rather skip the hard work of recovery? Yet growth involves moving through barriers and wading into dark places, not skipping around and pretending they aren't there. But tending to our souls isn't just up to us. God is the restorer of our souls who might make us lie down sometimes. God knows what we need and values our restoration, our healing, and our transformation. As the psalmist states,

> He makes me lie down in green pastures;
> he leads me beside still waters;
> he restores my soul. (Psalm 23:2-3)

Soul care doesn't just mean spiritual care. It means tending to our inner psychospiritual life, which affects our whole self. The Hebrew understanding of the self is holistic, with the body, soul, and spirit being interdependent. We are complex, intertwined beings, with our soul, body, mind, and emotions all amazingly interconnected.

Often I've been unaware of how stress impacts my body, not to mention my mind and emotions. I don't notice that I'm having trouble thinking clearly and am easily agitated. Acute stress is a natural physiological response derived from our flight, fight, and freeze survival responses. However, too much stress and prolonged chronic stress can have a negative impact on us.

When I was in the midst of burnout, my dentist took a look at my teeth and asked if I was stressed at work. He could see the effects of stress on my jaw and teeth. Understanding the multifaceted ways that stress impacts us can heighten our awareness of our stress levels and of our need to make changes.

Soul care doesn't necessarily involve self-care activities to add to our schedule but habits to break. It involves tools to extend empathy toward ourselves and to make us more grounded in our identity when we're feeling anxious. As I've begun to address the false beliefs that drive my unhealthy behaviors and integrate Centering Prayer as a daily practice, my whole self has benefited: I take bathroom and lunch breaks. I breathe easier and don't grind my teeth as much. I'm more grounded, less stressed, and more alive. I'm resilient and free to thrive. Soul care practices invite a new way of life—a life in recovery from addictions to workaholism and codependency.

Our soul care also equips us to love others from a healthier place; it doesn't just lead us inward. We're better able to do justice, love mercy, and walk humbly with our God (Micah 6:8). Pastors Reesheda Graham-Washington and Shawn Casselberry write about soul force, a philosophy of nonviolence rooted in the teaching of Jesus. Soul force "is not limited to personal spiritual growth alone; it transforms communities and social systems. Soul force creates an outward ripple effect, changing us and changing our world simultaneously." Just as Henri Nouwen emphasized movement from solitude to community to ministry, we first need to engage in inner work that grounds us in God. We are then able to connect to community from a healthier place. Rooted and held, we are better equipped for our work and ministry.

STEPPINGSTONES TO RESILIENCE AND THRIVING

Holistic, trauma-informed soul care practices are the steppingstones to resilience—our ability to bounce back in the face of trauma and other hardships. People who experience primary trauma and oppression have to learn to be resilient to survive. One purpose of this book is that we learn to become more resilient, adapting and flourishing in the face of adversity. It's *also* so we can thrive as beloved children of God, step into our calling, and know we are loved, no matter *what* we're doing or *how* we're doing.

It's becoming increasingly common to encourage practices that develop resilience. Rick Hanson, author of a number of books, including most recently *Resilient: How to Grow an Unshakable Core of Calm, Strength, and Happiness*, writes, "While resilience helps us to recover from loss and trauma, it offers us much more than that. True resilience fosters well-being, an underlying sense of happiness, love, and peace." Developing resilience is key to working sustainably with people who are experiencing trauma and to tending to the ongoing grief and triggers generated by our own trauma.

In addition, we need to recognize that being resilient in order to persevere in our work isn't always the key to thriving. Sometimes we need to make a dramatic change: quit our job. Years after burnout, I was working as a program manager for a youth residential facility. The job reality was far from the description portrayed in the interview process. The program, instead of being "smoothly running," was nonfunctional. There were no youth housed in the program due to insufficient staffing and failing to meet government standards. In order for it to reopen and begin hosting kids again, I spent the first few months hiring seven additional staff members and working as both the program manager and the mental health counselor.

It didn't take long to realize this wasn't sustainable for me. Though I believed deeply in the need to care for unaccompanied minors, the expectations for my work and the lack of organizational support were intolerable. The job wasn't about to change, and I realized if I were to thrive (let alone survive), I needed to quit, as heartbreaking as it was.

Sometimes we need to choose a new path. Maybe the path is a completely different trajectory. Founder and director of the Trauma Stewardship Institute Laura van Dernoot Lipsky invites workshop participants and readers to consider their plan B. I remember sitting in her class and thinking, "Hmm, my plan B is to work with survivors of trafficking." Then I heard her explain that a plan B isn't just a subtle shift, like working at a shelter for survivors of trafficking instead of for victims of domestic violence. It was like she read my mind: I was currently working at a local domestic violence shelter and wanting to work more with survivors of trafficking internationally.

At the time, I couldn't conceptualize *not* working directly with people in some form of advocacy or social-justice ministry. I found much of my identity in that kind of work, as it aligned with my passion, interests, and calling. I wanted to make a difference, and working with traumatized people was what I felt called to—and still do. These were valid reasons for doing that work, but I also needed to hear that I have value even if I don't work with people experiencing trauma. Suffice it to say, I'm still discovering my plan B.

I frequently go with my young daughter to visit the local aquarium. She delights in seeing the fish and watching the octopus, and she's gathering courage to touch the anemones. One day, as we watched a diver feed fish in a giant tank, I realized what might be obvious to others but was a truth I needed to realize: I could change my career and become an aquarium scuba diver, and God would still value me just as much.

RHYTHMS, RESOURCES, AND EXERCISES

Integrating life-giving rhythms is essential to rooting ourselves in God's truth and to building resilience. Having regular prayer practices is not a new concept. Monastic and other faith communities have practiced daily rhythms for millennia. These valued traditions have helped many connect with God and themselves.

We'll explore rhythms more in chapter thirteen, but for now, I invite you to choose at least one daily or weekly practice to integrate into your schedule.

How to start a daily practice. Explore what practice and timeframe works for you. The important thing is to do it daily and to make it simple enough to be attainable. It could be five to ten minutes of stillness, stretching, or listening to music at the beginning or end of the day. Ideally, choose a centering practice that grounds you in God and in your identity as beloved.

Weekly practice. You may already have a weekly practice; however, like other rhythms, it too gets brushed aside to allow for the "more urgent." As you read this book, consider what rejuvenating weekly practice you might want to include in your present season of life to nourish and bring you joy.

> *Because we do not rest, we lose our way. We miss the compass points that would show us where to go, we bypass the nourishment that would give us succor. We miss the quiet that would give us wisdom. We miss the joy and love born of effortless delight.*
> WAYNE MULLER

Exercises. At the end of each chapter, there are a few reflection questions, exercises, and recommended resources. I've included a variety to fit different personalities, seasons, and moods—from poems to YouTube videos to prayer exercises. These exercises aren't intended just to be things you have to check off your list. Instead they're offerings you can choose from to go deeper with God in your recovery. Choose one or two that stand out to you.

Hold your commitments with courage and give yourself grace. Remember that the best way to move toward change is through small steps, integrating a regular practice, and addressing your inner beliefs.

REFLECTION QUESTIONS

- What are your reasons for wanting holistic, trauma-informed soul care and for taking this journey?
- In what ways are you being invited to lie down? In what ways do you need rest and restoration?
- Take some time to consider how stress affects you. How does it affect your mind, body, and spirit? Where do you carry it in your body? In what ways does work-related stress affect your life out of work? How do you cope with stress?
- What is your plan B if you were to do something other than caregiving?

EXERCISES

- Consider Psalm 23:2-3: "He makes me lie down in green pastures; he leads me beside still waters; he restores my soul."
- Practice the five-minute Free-Write Exercise in appendix one.
- Watch Laura van Dernoot Lipsky's "Beyond the Cliff," TedX Talk, April 23, 2015.

RECOMMENDED RESOURCES

Soul Force: Seven Pivots toward Courage, Community, and Change by Reesheda Graham-Washington and Shawn Casselberry

The Artist's Way by Julia Cameron

People of Color Online Classroom, "Self-Care," www.poconlineclassroom.com/self-care

Headington Institute, headington-institute.org/overview, an online resource center providing resources on stress, resilience, and humanitarian work.

TWO

LIVING AS BELOVED

Self-rejection is the greatest enemy of the spiritual life because it contradicts the sacred voice that calls us the "beloved." Being the Beloved expresses the core truth of our existence.

HENRI NOUWEN, *LIFE OF THE BELOVED*

MOVING *FROM* BELOVEDNESS, NOT *FOR* BELOVEDNESS

When I look back at my journal entries, trying to understand what drove me to addictive behavior, I see common threads. Although I knew in my head that I was loved, I didn't allow that truth to impact my actions.

After finishing up a day at Tierra Nueva's Family Support Center, I often chose to spend time with the Martinez kids, who I knew through the ministry. The parents were working two seasonal farm jobs and making ends meet, and they welcomed me to the table and offered warm homemade tortillas whenever I dropped by. They loved coming to our ministry house and were a delight to have around. The kids usually requested grilled cheese sandwiches, watched *Mr. Bean*, and then ran around the house, playing hide and seek. With their parents' agreement, I often let them convince me to take them to my house for a couple of hours after school. Otherwise they returned alone to an empty house. I loved being with them, though I was often worn out from a long day.

One evening, after dropping them off at their house, I was exhausted and frustrated at my inability to know what I needed and to make good decisions. I yanked open my journal and wrote,

> What's wrong with me? I run and get addicted to busyness, adrenaline, and a fast pace of life. I have a hard time slowing down. I can't say no to good things and those in need. I don't want to disappoint people, so I just go without thinking critically and pack too much in. I need to move from "compulsion to contemplation." I need a healthy balance of contemplation and action.

Slowly I realized I hadn't taken time to center in God for a long time. My inability to say no and my busyness kept me in a vicious cycle. It was easier to say yes than to respond thoughtfully with *maybe*, *not now*, or *no*. I was aware that I needed to slow down and recenter, yet I had a hard time giving myself permission to do so. I was responding to people's requests, thinking I was being loving and sacrificial, yet sometimes I was perpetuating unhealthy dependency. (See chapter twelve for more on discerning when to say no and yes.)

A few days later, God whispered to my heart, "Bethany, you don't need to feel guilty for taking care of yourself, for not giving to others. You have such a giver mentality. It's not just okay to receive, but it's needed." God was inviting me to let go, receive, and be embraced. I began understanding the truth: I am loved regardless of what I do. I am also wounded and in need of healing.

When I take time for a daily practice, I am reoriented to the truth of my belovedness. I feel less anxious, more clearheaded, and better able to make thoughtful decisions not based on what others think of me. I respond with more grace to others and myself. I'm able to love myself more fully because I know God loves me. Seeing myself in God's eyes and receiving God's love for me helps me to extend it to others. I remember that I'm not important to God because God can work through me and help more people. I'm valued because God cares about me: my work, my relationships, and my well-being. I live knowing I *am* loved, instead of striving *to be* loved.

Being the beloved changes everything.

EMBRACING AN IDENTITY AS GOD'S BELOVED

As I've pursued this recovery journey, I've picked up books that have repulsed me but then surprised me with a few poignant truths. The front cover of one self-care book shows a white woman poised on a beach in a chunky sweater with her hair and makeup perfectly in place. Relaxation? Beauty? Embracing yourself? Self-care is only for wealthy white people? I'm not sure what the author was trying to communicate through that cover image, but it didn't appeal to me.

To improve self-love, the author encouraged readers to look at themselves in the mirror and say, "You're beautiful" and "I love you." While some might find this helpful, I find it challenging, if not ridiculous. I can't just talk myself into being loved. I don't want to stand in front of a mirror and speak to my reflection. It doesn't work for me. And yet, in spite of the silly cover and the unhelpful exercises, there is a core truth in the message: we need to know that we are loved.

Over the course of our lives, many of us ingest the message that we are loved *for what we do*. Instead of being nourished by God's voice of love and truth, many Christians feed on the same message of worth: we are conditioned to do "godly" work and burdened by the consequences of chronic guilt and shame. We're told that we can't have acceptance and love unless we are successful. A common get-to-know-you question in Western society is "What do you do?" But in many other cultures, people ask about family relations. For years, when people asked me what I did, I knew my answer would get some kind of praise. Unconsciously I felt gratified by this. I believed my life had meaning and purpose because of what I did. Yet I also let that impact my sense of self-worth.

The theology of original sin has also affected how we see ourselves and how we operate in the world. It says that we are fundamentally depraved or evil. Although we have the capacity to do evil, we are not evil. We are wounded and in need of healing. Pastor Danielle Shroyer writes that we need a theology of original blessing. "Original blessing reminds us that God calls us *good* and *beloved* before we are anything else. Sin is not at the heart of our nature; blessing is. And that didn't stop being true because Adam and Eve ate fruit in the garden. In fact, it has never stopped being true." The good news is not that we are sinful and separated from God, but that God pursued us by becoming human.

Countless other messages pervade our society, attempting to dictate our worth. God breaks into our world so we might be whole and experience the fullness of life that we're created for. We're beloved at our core, no matter what mistakes we make or what trauma we experience. Years ago, I read another book that I've since read countless times: Henri Nouwen's *Life of the Beloved*. He beautifully articulates an essential truth that I need to hear over and over again: "I am a beloved daughter of God." This truth is based not just in my perception of myself or my claims that I am loved, but on the fact that I am and always will be profoundly loved by God. It contradicts the messages that tell me I'm loved because of what

I do, what I have, or what others say about me. What we do doesn't give us additional worth. As Danielle Shroyer wrote, "Who we are, before anything else, more than anything else, is children of God."

Although God does work through us and chooses to partner with us, God doesn't just want to "use" us for the kingdom. We are not just means to an end. We are called friends, not servants (John 15:15).

Even Jesus received and lived out of his identity as beloved. His identity as "beloved Son" is declared three times: at his baptism, at the transfiguration, and as fulfillment of Isaiah's prophecy. In each of these accounts, the Father declared variations of this: "This is my beloved son, in whom I am well pleased" (Matthew 3:17; 12:18; 17:5). These words were first spoken over Jesus at his baptism, before he performed any miracles that we know of. He hadn't done anything to achieve his belovedness. He was called *beloved* before he publicly ministered to others. Jesus let this identity be the core of who he was.

Over and over and over, Scripture assures us we are loved. In Song of Solomon alone, the word *beloved* is mentioned twenty-five times, perhaps referring to human love, perhaps in an allegory that reflects the love between God and God's people. Throughout the Bible, the word *beloved* is used to refer to all of God's people, whether by God toward people (in Nehemiah, Isaiah, Psalms) or by others speaking to God's people. The apostle Paul repeatedly addresses followers of Jesus as "beloved," writing, "To all God's beloved in Rome, who are called to be saints" (Romans 1:7).

We are precious in God's sight and carriers of God's presence. Our bodies are holy, referred to as "God's temple" (2 Corinthians 6:16). God lives in us, walks with us, and calls us beloved people (vv. 15-17). We are invited to turn toward love and away from fear, because we know who we are, because we belong.

Knowing we are beloved and that our bodies matter empowers us to take better care of ourselves. It isn't a fear tactic to do more self-care but a reorientation of our basis for worth and belonging. We don't have to work to belong. We already do. We are created as good and called by name.

> *Do not fear, for I have redeemed you; I have called you by name, you are mine.*
> ISAIAH 43:1

We have a normal and healthy need to know we are loved and to be loved. Yet perhaps you, like me, fight being beloved, seek people's affirmations, and set unrealistic expectations for yourself that you think you must meet before you can be lovable. You forgive others yet aren't able to forgive yourself. You love to help others sacrificially yet resist receiving help.

Living as beloved involves learning to receive and extend love to ourselves. We can give away only what we receive. Jesus declared that the second most important thing we do is to "love your neighbor as yourself" (Matthew 22:39). How can we love others if we don't love ourselves? To do our work as social workers, pastors, and caregivers, we need to serve others from this position of knowing our identity as beloved children. We also need to let ourselves be loved, even though we aren't perfect.

RECEIVING GOD'S DELIGHT

We might conceptually know that God loves us yet have a harder time knowing that God likes and even delights in us. For six years, I led regular dialogical Bible studies in a local women's jail. The majority of women were in for drug-related offenses. They were experiencing significant withdrawals and facing the rawness of emotions that drugs had squelched. They often felt rejected by family, society, and God—assuming God had also turned God's back. Witnessing them experience God's welcoming radical love made me a believer all over again.

One Sunday, I shared with the women my fresh amazement that God delights in us as well as the parallel invitation to delight in God. I invited them to think about and share their thoughts on these questions:

- How do you think God sees and feels about you?
- What are some words you think God would use to describe you?
- When you think about God, what do you feel?

The women gave a variety of responses. Some truly believed God loved them and was there for them. Others shared that they believed God loved them because God had to. They expressed feeling like "damaged goods" or "stray dogs," and they thought God saw them the same way. How could God truly love them when they'd hurt and disappointed so many people close to them?

For the mothers, the pain of being separated from their kids was palpable. Most prayer requests and tears were for their kids. Whether separated by Child Protective Services, by jail time, or by family interventions, every mother I ever met expressed grief at the impact of her behavior on her kids. So many of the women felt unlovable and unforgivable.

Together we read a number of passages about delight, including this verse: "He brought me out into a broad place; he delivered me, because he delighted in me" (Psalm 18:19). Sparks enlivened their eyes as they began to catch glimmers of the extravagant grace and abundant love of God. God rescues us because God delights in us—not because we are clean and sober, have it all together, or haven't made any mistakes. As expressed by nineteenth-century missionary Amy Carmichael: "There is no need to plead that the love of God shall fill our hearts as though He were unwilling to fill us. . . . Love is pressing around us on all sides like air. Cease to resist it and instantly love takes possession."

As we closed our time together in the jail, I invited the women to receive more of God's love, asking them to open their hands as a symbol of acceptance. Women whose hands had known drug injections, abuse, and handcuffs opened to receive God's love and embrace—a God who tears through heaven and earth to lift them up from the miry pit, a God whose hands were also bound and who experienced violence.

We watch as our hearts begin to beat as one with the One who delights in our being.
FATHER GREG BOYLE

Whether we are incarcerated by jail walls, or by societal structures, or by inner walls that keep us from believing we are loved, God loves us no matter what. God doesn't love us for the good that we do as ministers, therapists, or social workers. We're invited to step down from thinking that we need to be the "expert caregiver" and recognize that we are all dependent, broken, and in need of God. God rescues and is with us, because God delights in us.

To receive God's delight and love myself, I've needed to not just to tell myself "I love you," but also to open my hands and say yes to God's work in me. I've needed to go behind the inner walls and discover the disturbed and wounded areas. To be honest, even writing "love myself" still seems cheesy. I have resistance.

We will unpack such barriers in more depth in the following chapters. For now, spend some time listening to God, prayerfully asking the following questions.

REFLECTION QUESTIONS

- What is your identity and worth based on? Who tries to define you?

- How does this affect how you take care of yourself and interact with others or with God?
- Consider asking God, how does God see and feel about you? When you think about God, what do you feel?
- How has your view of how God sees you impacted your sense of calling?

EXERCISES

- Develop a breath prayer or daily prayer. (See appendix one.)
- Learn from Prison Contemplative Fellowship or Contemplative Outreach about Centering Prayer as a way to practice being still in God's presence.
- Listen to "Becoming the Beloved" by Graham Cooke (a YouTube series).
- Consider this poem, "Laughter Came From Every Brick," by St. Teresa of Avila.

Just these two words He spoke
changed my life,
"Enjoy me."
What a burden I thought I was to carry—
a crucifix, as did He.
Love once said to me, "I know a song,
would you like to hear it?"
And laughter came from every brick in the street
and from every pore
in the sky.
After a night of prayer, He
changed my life when
He sang,
"Enjoy Me."

RECOMMENDED RESOURCES

Invited: Simple Prayer Exercises for Solitude and Community by Lorie Martin

This Day: Collected and New Sabbath Poems by Wendell Berry

Life of the Beloved by Henri Nouwen

Finding God Within by Ray Leonardini

THREE

WOUNDED HEALERS

The soul would have no rainbows if the eyes had no tears.

NATIVE AMERICAN PROVERB

Our team of jail chaplains tells the women in jail, "Call us when you get out. We're excited to see you! We want to hang out, get coffee. It doesn't matter if you are using; just call us. We care about you." Yet only a few women have taken us up on the offer. Some are immediately caught up again in cycles of addiction, and we see them months or years later in jail. Others we never hear from. Perhaps they make changes for the better; perhaps they spiral deeper into addiction.

While in jail, most women acknowledge their brokenness and hurt. Seeds of change and transformation start to grow again. Sometimes, due to lack of access to drugs, emotions previously buried come rushing to the surface, yet many women don't have the tools to navigate them.

Tender shoots of new life begin to rise. As chaplains, we hope to accompany the women after they're released, knowing it's hard to stick with recovery. We hate seeing them caught in addiction, and we long for them to answer texts. We fight to counter their shame, wanting them to know how beloved they are—no matter what.

For one woman I cared deeply about over the years, I was actually grateful when I'd see her name on the jail roster. Not that I wanted her to be there; it just meant she was alive and I'd be able to find her. While in jail, she'd share vulnerably and eagerly about her desire to change. We'd make plans to meet up after she got out. I'd wait at Tierra Nueva during our chosen time, and she wouldn't come. She wouldn't answer my texts. Once I waited for her outside the jail, only to find out she had been released a few hours earlier when it was a more convenient time for the guards. Those few hours meant despair and a quick, easy walk to the nearest dealer. I asked others about her and tried to get the message to her that I'd love to see her, no matter what.

I've come to believe that, in the same way, God loves it when I show up and am willing to receive help. *Here I am Lord. I can't do this on my own. Can you help me?* I imagine that, like I do with the women, God watches me return to unhealthy habits, not pursuing and prioritizing life-giving habits. How often has God wanted to hold me in my brokenness, seeing me with love and compassion—and yet I have run. I have denied my wounds, been caught in my addictions, and based my worth on the perspectives of others.

God pursues us with arms wide open, saying, "When you are ready, I am here. I can't want your transformation more than you do or more than you're ready for. I see that you're stuck in unhealthy patterns. I'm eager to tend to your wounds, to meet you in your brokenness, to throw you a banqueting party. Yet without your willingness to receive, I won't force myself on you." Acknowledging our brokenness opens up a way for God to move, healing and liberating us from unhealthy habits.

The Enneagram, a model of personality types and styles, helped reveal my deeper wounding. If it's not clear yet, I'm predominantly what the Enneagram calls type two: a helper. Pride is named as our root sin. At first this came as a surprise. I thought I was self-sacrificial, yet I was actually prideful, thinking that I "had it all together" or at least needed to have it all together. As I dug deeper and let Jesus speak to me, I realized how often pride creeps into my ways of thinking and behaving. It's pride that keeps me spinning in the hamster wheel. It's pride that causes my dislike of being needy and even of being aware of my needs. It's pride that drives my codependency—a relationship addiction to meeting our needs. (I'll share more about that later.)

Claiming that we are loved by God doesn't mean we think we're perfect. In fact, it recognizes that we aren't perfect: we are wounded *and* we are loved. Our wounds differ depending on our personality, socioeconomic status, race, gender, sexuality, family stories, nationality, and ethnicity. Our wounds are not the same shape or dimension. But it's impossible to encounter another without our wounds.

Many are driven to choose counseling and advocacy work because of wounds, both past and present. According to one study, personal trauma motivates the majority of helping professionals to choose their career, as they want to advocate for and accompany people who have experienced similar trauma. Initially coined by Carl Jung, the term "wounded healer" now refers to all professional healers who have been psychologically wounded.

As we care for others, we often come face to face with our own wounds and powerlessness. We might be tempted to be ashamed and to hide because of our wounds, or to let them tell us we are bad. Yet, as Danielle Shroyer wrote in *Original Blessing*, asking for healing and help is not saying we are bad, but that something is wrong. Sin attacks our health and well-being. And since sin makes us sick, we need a healer. We need Jesus. Shroyer also wrote, "Like an infection, [sin] shows us that something isn't working properly. . . . Illness isn't meant to be our nature. Health is."

We're invited to recognize our sickness and to ask for help. This is core to the journey of recovery. It's actually the first step of any twelve-step program. We need to admit that we don't have it all together; we need Jesus and others.

Areas of weakness can become fault lines when we experience or live with a high level of stress. They can also become gifts through which we gain compassion and are drawn into greater dependence on each other and on the One we serve. My hope is that as we explore our areas of wounding and weakness, we are more aware of our inner struggles and become receptive to change.

A deep understanding of [our] own pain makes it possible for [us] to convert [our] weakness into strength and to offer [our] own experience as a source of healing.

HENRI NOUWEN

When acknowledged, our wounds can be vessels for healing. We get to follow Jesus, who makes his "own broken body the way to health, to liberation and new life," as Henri Nouwen wrote in his book *The Wounded Healer*. "Thus like Jesus, he who proclaims liberation is called not only to care for his own wounds and the wounds of others, but also to make his wounds into a major source of his healing power." People often say that hurting people hurt people. Healing people also heal people. Our greatest burden can become the source of our greatest gift.

Knowing ourselves—our triggers, weaknesses, gifts, and desires—leads to more fruitful encounters with others and equips us to take better care of ourselves. Psychologist David Benner wrote, "What I have to give to others is directly proportional to the extent of my genuine and deep knowing of myself. . . . [To] the extent that I am genuinely and deeply congruent, authentic and my true or real self, others who meet me are afforded an opportunity to be a true or real self themselves." Whether we know it or not, how we listen and speak is often impacted by what is going on inside of us. When I'm grounded in my identity as beloved, I interact differently with others. When I'm rested and supported, I'm more present and able to listen well. Knowing and living into our true selves can also inspire the same in others.

In contrast, if we don't do our own inner work, if we let our wounds fester unattended or allow them to remain in our subconscious, we live and give out of our false self. Our false self, often called the shadow self or ego, is the part of us created mostly during our childhood as a way to understand and survive in the world and to meet our basic needs. It may have developed to survive in a toxic environment. It encompasses our beliefs and often drives our feelings and behaviors without our knowledge.

My false self is anxious, insecure, and in need of people's affirmation and approval. I readily say yes out of a need for approval instead of discerning a right and helpful response. As I receive God's love, I'm able to accept myself and to live into my true self. I'm also freed from compulsive behavior. I don't exist just to help others, to serve others, or to change the world.

Benner says that knowing ourselves in connection to God involves knowing three things: we are deeply loved, we are broken, and we are in the process of restoration. "Facing these deep truths about ourselves makes it possible for us to accept and know ourselves as we are accepted and known by God." We are invited to consent to and to receive God's work in us, yet we aren't able to "fix" ourselves. Our healing, growth, and restoration is not just up to us; God is the author and healer.

> *Blessed be the God and Father of our Lord Jesus Christ, the Father of mercies and the God of all consolation, who consoles us in all our affliction, so that we may be able to console those who are in any affliction with the consolation with which we ourselves are consoled by God.*
>
> 2 CORINTHIANS 1:3-4

In our work as helping professionals, we're often inviting—if not asking—people to be vulnerable and encouraging them to live out of their true selves. By doing our own work to understand ourselves as beloved *and broken* children, we can authentically practice the same vulnerability, being aware of our limits and ongoing healing journeys. In the next section, we will start by unpacking our internal barriers.

REFLECTION QUESTIONS

- How do you view your woundedness? How has it motivated you in your choice of profession?
- What steps have you already taken to move toward healing?

EXERCISES

- Listen to the song "Brokenness Aside" by Sons and Daughters.
- Try the Free-Write Exercise in appendix one. Continue free-writing with different prompts such as what are my likes, dislikes, needs, desires, values, or dreams?
- Learn about your Enneagram personality type through reading, listening to podcasts, or attending a workshop.

RECOMMENDED RESOURCES

The Wounded Healer by Henri Nouwen

Made for Goodness by Archbishop Desmond Tutu and Mpho Tutu

The Gift of Being Yourself: The Sacred Call to Self-Discovery by David Benner

Atlas: Enneagram, an album by Sleeping at Last

Unorthodoxy Podcast: Enneagram by Duncan Reyburn

Healing the Healers (healingthehealers.org), a media resource intended to support clergy, laity, social workers, first responders and other spiritual care providers facing community-level trauma.

PART TWO

UNPACKING

To see the possibility of our freedom, we must see the contours of our bondage.

DR. BRIAN BANTUM

FOUR

SECONDARY TRAUMA

Trauma response becomes hard to assess because of the day-in, day-out toll or accumulative toll; however, it doesn't need to become accumulative trauma.

LAURA VAN DERNOOT LIPSKY, *TRAUMA STEWARDSHIP*

Learning about how trauma was affecting me was instrumental in finding a new path forward. I mentioned previously that I didn't realize how much I was being affected by trauma until I had to take an emergency week off and make significant changes. I was weary even after eight hours of sleep. I also began noticing how part of my busyness was because I didn't want to slow down long enough to think about the stories and tragedies I faced. I made myself feel better by doing something productive and helping others. Saying I was a codependent social-justice workaholic might be an understatement.

Secondary trauma is a byproduct of the helping profession and not something to feel ashamed about. When firefighters go into a burning house, they come out covered with ash. In a similar way, we are affected when we work with people who are experiencing trauma. Even just hearing about trauma can lead to symptoms similar to post-traumatic stress disorder.

PERVASIVE TRAUMA EXPOSURE

Many helping professionals experience trauma vicariously through hearing stories at work. Some carry prior trauma; they know what it's like to flee a burning house. Many also experience everyday oppression based on their racial, ethnic, sexual, or gender identity. They feel like they're living in a burning house.

For people of color, trauma is repeatedly experienced through fear of direct assaults and microaggressions. Spiritual director and therapist Sheila Wise Rowe wrote that microaggression is "the lobbed grenade that creates damage because it comes when least expected and sends a message that we are alien." *Microaggression* is too minimal a word according to Ibram X. Kendi. He writes, "I detest its component parts—'micro' and 'aggression.' A persistent daily low hum of racist abuse is not minor. . . . Abuse accurately describes the action and its effects on people: distress, anger, worry, aggression, anxiety, pain, fatigue, and suicide." Reeling from racist abuse, a clinician may be sitting safely in a chair, listening to someone else's story, yet carrying the stress and reliving the smells and sounds of an encounter earlier that morning.

Rowe also described the vicarious trauma she experienced as a person of color due to the onslaught of news about Black people being gunned down, especially after the 2016 elections. She wrote, "I was anxious for the safety of my Black son and husband. *What if there is a traffic stop or a case of mistaken identity?* My emotions were a crescendo of anger, denial, sadness, resignation, indifference, cynicism about reconciliation, and bone-tiredness that ebbed or flowed at the latest slight or all-out assault on other people of color and me." Vicarious trauma didn't stop after she finished meeting with her last client, because hearing about traumatic realities is not confined to a clinical setting; it pervades conversations and experiences at home, on the bus, and at places as seemingly innocuous as the grocery store.

Trauma affects our capacity to make sense of the world, overwhelming our senses and wrecking our previous understandings of the world, of ourselves, and often of God. Theologian Serene Jones wrote, "Like the wave of a tsunami, [traumatic events] drown you and disable your normal strategies for dealing with difficulties. . . . They override your powers of both action and imagination." Even our ability to make sense of trauma is thwarted. As our "self-esteem is assaulted by experiences of humiliation, guilt, and helplessness," we lose trust in ourselves, in others, and in God. Extending grace to ourselves is essential as we face horrific realities and grapple with our own trauma and triggers.

WORK-RELATED FACTORS

When I was in the midst of unhealthy workplace dynamics, I barely noticed them. In my assortment of social work and ministry jobs, our staff meetings hardly ever included opportunities—let alone encouragement—to share how we were being affected by people's stories. My meetings as a social worker centered on case consults. In ministry, our concern for each other was expressed as we prayed with and for each other. But we usually told success stories regarding advocating for change and the challenges experienced by people we accompanied. We were there to help, to be strong, capable, and unaffected. If I was being impacted by people's traumatic realities, that was my fault; being affected was equated with weakness. Such a sentiment contributes to the belief that any emotional exhaustion and burnout was because of a personal internal flaw. As a result if we think we're struggling because of our limited capacity or inabilities, we're likely to blame ourselves if we burn out.

Burnout can occur solely because of secondary trauma, and yet it's often compounded by organizational culture and work-related stress. Christina Maslach, creator of the widely used Maslach Burnout Inventory, defines burnout as a "syndrome of emotional exhaustion, depersonalization, and reduced personal accomplishment that can occur among individuals who do 'people work' of some kind. It's a response to the chronic emotional strain of dealing extensively with other human beings, particularly when they are troubled or having problems." Another phrase used to describe this emotional exhaustion is "compassion fatigue." It affects our ability to do our work effectively, think critically, and maintain boundaries.

We associate success with how dependable and available we are. And before we know it, success and burnout become one and the same.

SAYU BHOJWANI

As mentioned previously, white-dominated environments contribute to emotional exhaustion. Austin Channing Brown powerfully described the emotional labor and toll: "It's work to be the only person of color in an organization, bearing the weight of all of your white co-workers' questions about Blackness. . . . The work isn't just tedious. It can be dangerous for Black women to attempt to carve out space for themselves . . . in places that haven't examined the prevailing assumptions of white culture." The stress and challenge of navigating white-dominated environments can not only increase the likelihood of burnout but also be traumatic for people of color.

Moral injury creates an added dynamic in many settings. Although moral injury is most often spoken of in the context of war, the term is also prevalent in helping professions. Moral injury is the "damage done to one's conscience or moral compass when that person perpetrates, witnesses, or fails to prevent acts that transgress one's own moral beliefs, values, or ethical codes of conduct. . . . [It] is damage done to the soul of the individual." It arises from the challenge of denying care to someone in need because of organizational policy, such as not being able to respond adequately to a suicidal client; of failing to provide the desired level of medical care due to job restraints and paperwork; or of a church's failure to create bridges instead of deny racism. Due to moral injury, physicians are not just burning out; they are committing suicide at twice the rate of active duty military members.

Secondary trauma, moral injury, and other work-related stressors can lead to compassion fatigue and significant health challenges. We may experience a combination or one but not the others. I experienced burnout largely as a result of compassion fatigue and secondary trauma. However, the further away I am from my burnout, the more I realize the role organizational culture played in it.

After taking Lipsky's "Self-Care for Social Workers" class, I realized I wasn't alone. My responses were not only normal but also were linked to the chaotic and traumatic realities I was witnessing. I asked my supervisors for space within staff meetings to share about how we were doing, and I began to hear common threads.

To move toward resilience and recovery, we need to recognize the impact of secondary trauma and to extend compassion to ourselves. By creating opportunities to share among colleagues, we can help each other notice our trauma exposure responses and to journey together toward healthier rhythms and boundaries.

FEELING GUILTY AND OVERWHELMED

For many years, I've carried a strong sense of guilt for my privilege, granted to me for being white, American, middle class, able-bodied, heterosexual, cisgender, educated, and growing up in a healthy two-parent home. Unconsciously I've wondered, *How can I rest or do something fun when so many people I know are suffering so much and barely surviving?*

Working at a domestic violence shelter, I downplayed any goodness I experienced. Women would casually ask me about my life or how my weekend went. No matter how it was, I would say "fine" or "I'm okay." I didn't give myself permission to express my enjoyment of healthy relationships and activities. I was surprised when I read in Lipsky's book of another domestic violence advocate responding the same way.

The needs of those around us can quickly supersede the attention we give to our own care. We minimize our suffering compared to others. If we feel guilty for taking time off, we don't take time off, and as a result, risk burning out.

Guilt doesn't help anyone; it negatively affects not only us but also others. Brown described the experience of receiving white-privilege guilt as "having tar dry all over your hands and heart." For this reason, Lipsky rightly calls guilt "toxic." She also uses the term *frumpify* to refer to how shelter staff dress down unconsciously because of a fear of looking too nice or making people jealous.

> *If the therapist's bystander guilt is not properly understood and contained, she runs the risk of ignoring her own legitimate interests. In the therapy relationship she may assume too much personal responsibility for the patient's life, thus once again patronizing and disempowering the patient.*
>
> **JUDITH HERMAN**

Not all resonate with this, but I sure did. Did I think the women would feel better about their lives if I was also miserable? Did I think denying my guilt or privilege would benefit others? I share about past guilt not to add further tar, but in the hope of revealing the ways it blocked me from health and from loving those around me.

I had fallen into the trap of believing that I don't *deserve* to enjoy goodness. Although I want to reduce my consumption, doing my part to steward the earth's resources and being sensitive to vast socioeconomic inequities, joy isn't a consumable resource. Perhaps honoring my story and who I am, expressing freely that I had a lovely weekend, might actually give others hope. In fact, I never sensed any resentment from women in the shelter. They often encouraged me and were excited to hear any good news. In being fully and truly ourselves, we don't take away from others—in fact, we may help others know that goodness is possible.

Feeling guilty because we believe we don't deserve time off is one of Lipsky's *16 Warning Signs of a Trauma Exposure Response.* Another one is the "sense that one can never do enough." Depending on caregivers' personalities and life experiences, a multitude of other beliefs may drive their guilt. It's easy to have a sense that we're failing and terrible at the core, and in turn to feel guilty for anything we do for ourselves. Seeing guilt as a trauma warning sign can help us to put our behavior into context and to recognize our false beliefs, which we'll explore more in chapter seven.

For me, guilt doesn't just stem from my privilege; I tend to feel guilty for doing anything for myself. After quitting the very challenging program manager job at the shelter for undocumented children, I took some time off the following week. One day I decided to go to my family's cabin on a nearby lake for a day of solitude, reflection, and prayer. Before I left, I was unconsciously feeling guilty that I was taking time off while my husband was heading to his classes. Because I was feeling bad, I kept apologizing and asking if he was all right with it. He reminded me that he chose to take the classes, he was glad he is taking them, and he was more than happy that I was taking time away. In no way was he upset or jealous. Although I know he loves me and wants me to thrive, my fear and shame led me to feel guilty and to take responsibility for his emotions and actions. Now I clearly see the erroneous thinking. If I had started that day still consumed by guilt, I wouldn't have enjoyed it.

Although our actions affect each other, we aren't in control of anyone else's emotions. Although there is always more to do, guilt can drive us to take unhealthy responsibility for the well-being of others. In fact, this perception of being in control is one of the marks of codependency, which we will explore in the following chapter.

REFLECTION QUESTIONS

- In what ways do you experience guilt?
- How does guilt affect your ability to take care of yourself?
- What are some of the ways that you are affected by secondary trauma exposure?

EXERCISES

- Practice a grounding exercise by doing some free-writing or taking a Five Senses Walk (see appendix one; more on Five Senses Walks in chapter fourteen).
- Consider taking the Professional Quality of Life (ProQOL) screening. This is an assessment for helping professionals to gain a sense of their compassion fatigue, burnout, and compassion satisfaction, or the "pleasure you derive from being able to do your work well." Go to www.proqol.org/ProQol_Test.html.

RECOMMENDED RESOURCES

Trauma Stewardship: An Everyday Guide to Caring for Self While Caring for Others by Laura van Dernoot Lipsky and Connie Burk

Healing Racial Trauma: The Road to Resilience by Sheila Wise Rowe

Trauma and Recovery: The Aftermath of Violence—From Domestic Abuse to Political Terror by Judith Herman

The Compassion Fatigue Workbook: Creative Tools for Transforming Compassion Fatigue and Vicarious Traumatization by Françoise Mathieu

FIVE

CODEPENDENCY IN THE WORKPLACE

Codependency studies made us aware that much love is actually not love at all, but its most clever and bogus disguise. So much that is un-love and non-love, and even manipulative "love," cannot be seen or addressed because it is so dang sacrificial.

FR. RICHARD ROHR, *BREATHING UNDER WATER*

A few years ago, our pastoral advocacy team went above and beyond helping a woman who was living outside and just a few days clean from drugs. We asked permission for Clarice to stay in our main ministry building, which was not a frequent event. We promised that staff would be with her overnight. As we hurriedly explored next steps, a coworker found an amazing opportunity for her that provided housing and a job. It was out of town, away from fellow users and dealers. Perfect! She said she wanted it, and a day later moved into the motel where she would be cleaning, right next to the restaurant where she would be waitressing.

It seemed like a great fit. Staff visited Clarice regularly, providing support and encouragement. Two weeks later, we drove an hour to pick her up for church. But instead of sticking around after church and getting a ride back to the motel, she ran. She didn't return to our ministry and avoided our calls and messages for a long time. Was the change too much, too soon? Was she not ready? Perhaps.

I've had to learn that I can't want change more than others want it for themselves. Although I can provide support and accompany people to appointments, I'm powerless over them and their choices. Even if I think I see what needs to change or how their lives might improve, I can't make them change, nor is it ultimately my responsibility. Deciding for them instead of with them can actually be dehumanizing and disempowering.

The pain I feel watching people suffer with and battle addiction has often propelled me to act without considering what's manageable for the person. I've often thought that if they would just follow through with that housing appointment, go to court, make that first payment to get their license back, or show up for a CPS visitation meeting with their kids then their life would be better. But I'm not the expert in their story nor the change-maker. I often forget to be patient and to love them where they are. My own discomfort and desire for restoration cannot be my standard for helping someone.

Now I wonder if our compassion *and* our anxiety about Clarice made us rush her into a job and housing situation so *we* would feel better. Did it make us blind to the barriers and to her level of readiness to change?

People in helping professions are familiar with codependency among the people they work with—primarily recognizing it in relationships that are caught in cycles of domestic violence. However, it can be hard to see our own patterns of codependency in the work environment. Melody Beattie, author of *Codependent No More*, reveals that codependency is more common among people who are in relationship—whether personal or professional—with people in crisis.

RELATIONSHIP ADDICTION TO MEET OUR NEEDS

Codependency is a relationship addiction. It's an excessive and unhealthy responsibility for another person's life to the point of needing to control them, especially the part of life that the codependent person deems out of control. We have a hard time being at peace when others are not at peace, so we try to make them better—not for their well-being but for ours.

Codependency may look like trying to create peace, but it actually maintains a false peace. The codependent person demonstrates this through a desire to make everything okay. There may be a temptation to rush in to resolve or fix things. Someone in recovery or who has experienced trauma isn't going to be okay for a season. Pretending that others are okay when they aren't leads to inappropriate and even harmful responses. The prophet Jeremiah cried out against this false peace, saying,

> They dress the wound of my people
> as though it were not serious.
> "Peace, peace," they say,
> when there is no peace. (Jeremiah 6:14 NIV)

Although the desire for peace is healthy, seeking harmony and peace above all else can become toxic. We can't try to make situations and people better before they're ready.

Our own angst at seeing someone in pain may drive our actions, instead of us being led by God. We're invited to grieve with and not try to fix others. Father Greg Boyle, a Jesuit priest and the founder and director of Homeboy Industries in Los Angeles, beautifully writes about the "no matter whatness" and wholehearted, "full-throttle" compassion of God. Reflecting on the "slow work" of ministry, Father Greg said, "I've come to trust the value of simply showing up. . . . And yet, each time I find myself sitting with the pain that folks carry, I'm overwhelmed with my own inability to do much more than stand in awe, dumbstruck by the sheer size of the burden—more than I've ever been asked to carry." We stand in bewilderment with another, hold space for questions, and avoid rushing to solve or to soothe.

Codependency might be disguised as rescuing or saving another. Aside from certain professions that do perform rescue operations, a belief that it's our role to rescue another can easily turn into a messiah complex. Father Greg has also been impacted by the realities around him and the desire to save people. He wrote,

> In my early, crazy days doing this work with gangs, I will admit I was totally out of whack. I'd ride my bike, in the middle of the night, in the projects, trying to put out fires. . . . Trying to "save lives" is much like the guy spinning plates on *Ed Sullivan*, attempting to keep them from crashing to the floor. I'd look for the wobblers. Who was about to smash into a million pieces?—and then I'd be frantic to keep that homie from self-destructing. It was crazy-making, and I came close to the sun, to the immolation that comes from burning out completely in the delusion of actually "saving" people.

This rescuing mentality turns toxic for both the caregivers and the ones receiving care. The people who are receiving care feel helpless, disempowered, and possibly resentful. The caregivers feel overwhelmed and stressed out, and out of touch with how their frantic pace is affecting themselves or others. What changed for

Father Greg was taking a break from ministry and surrendering the work to God. He wrote, "I found consolation in a no doubt apocryphal story of Pope John XXIII. Apparently, at night he'd pray: 'I've done everything I can today for your church. But it's Your church, and I'm going to bed.'" Engaging in this work involves entrusting people to God.

Codependency is a way we meet our needs and desires—like the desire to create peace, be compassionate, and rescue someone. Our ability to recognize codependency is sometimes obscured by these healthy and admirable desires. As with all addictions, it's helpful to examine how we benefit from a certain behavior so we can move toward recovery. Codependency helps us avoid our own pain, helplessness, and fear by focusing our energy elsewhere. It pushes away our deeper fears and thoughts. Psychiatrist and trauma expert Judith Herman writes, "As a defense against the unbearable feeling of helplessness, the therapist may try to assume the role of a rescuer."

Codependency gives us a sense of worth, control, and purpose. It provides a meaningful identity; we view ourselves as "good people" or "helpers." Taking care of others is culturally rewarded and looks "godly" and compassionate. According to Co-Dependents Anonymous, one of the patterns of codependents is "perceive[ing] themselves as completely unselfish and dedicated to the well-being of others." Without naming it relationship addiction or codependency, Dietrich Bonhoeffer very clearly articulated the dynamics and consequences of a controlling and self-serving love.

> Human love is directed to the other person for his own sake, spiritual love loves him for Christ's sake. Therefore human love . . . wants to gain, to capture by every means; it uses force. It desires to be irresistible, to rule . . . even when it seems to be serving. . . . Spiritual love, however, comes from Jesus

> Christ, it serves him alone; it knows that it has no immediate access to other persons . . . spiritual love does not desire but rather serves.

We may think we're serving others, but in reality we're seeking to meet our own needs and desires. In contrast, codependents who are in recovery know "the difference between caring and caretaking . . . [and] recognize that caretaking others is often motivated by a need to benefit myself."

Like workaholism, codependency is often overlooked because it's societally and organizationally accepted. Father Richard Rohr wrote, "There are shared and agreed-upon addictions in every culture and every institution. These are often the hardest to heal because they do not look like addictions because we have all agreed to be compulsive about the same things and blind to the same problems."

Addictions sneak up on us without us realizing it. Stress, exhaustion, guilt, and fear can keep us in unhealthy and self-perpetuating cycles. We work long hours, not just because of financial need but also because we feel responsible. We get exhausted and stressed, which diminishes our ability to think creatively and to respond out of a place of peace and health. We fear letting people down or worry about what they think, so we work harder, with less boundaries and self-awareness. We feel unable to slow down, to recognize what's going on in us, and to take care of ourselves.

Staying busy can be a way of numbing ourselves. As I wrote earlier, my busyness kept me from grappling with the tragedies around me. Brené Brown describes this numbing as "living so hard and fast that the truths of our lives can't catch up with us. We fill every ounce of white space with something so there's no room or time for emotion to make itself known." She continued by writing, "If we numb compulsively and chronically—it's addiction."

We'll continue to explore how our needs and desires drive us and how to get out of those cycles more in the coming chapters.

EMPATHY WITHOUT GETTING HIJACKED

Codependency is different from being affected by the work we do. It's normal and healthy to be affected by our work and by people's challenging realities. In fact, it has been shown that a part of our brain responds to how another is acting and feeling. In 1994, Italian scientists discovered some specialized cells in the prefrontal cortex that have become known as mirror neurons. These neurons explain how, as Dr. Bessel van der Kolk writes,

> We pick up not only another person's movement but her emotional state and intentions as well. . . . Our mirror neurons also make us vulnerable to others' negativity, so that we respond to their anger with fury or are dragged down by their depression. . . . Treatment [of traumatized people] needs to reactivate the capacity to safely mirror, to be mirrored by others, but also to resist being hijacked by others' negative emotions.

For recovering codependents, it's easy to get "hijacked by others' negative emotions." One afternoon, when I was working for Tierra Nueva as a pastoral advocate, I received a frantic call from a woman I know well. Angie was calling me with a flat tire on the side of the freeway, with three of her five kids in the car, and late to pick up her two other kids from school. Understandably she was stressed and anxious. I took on her stress and made it mine. I was supposed to be meeting my then fiancé, and it was outside my normal work hours (albeit flexible pastoral advocacy hours).

Knowing she was in need, I didn't think twice about responding. I didn't slow down, take a breath, or think critically. I grabbed my stuff and quickly rushed to pick up my fiancé, barging in the door and saying, "We have to go now! We need to pick up Angie and her kids on the freeway."

He was understandably bewildered and asking questions, which of course I didn't have time to answer. I'm sure I didn't explain myself very well, as I was very sped up. We rushed off to meet Angie and pick up her three kids.

Although I still could have responded to her crisis, I didn't need to become consumed by it. Afterward my fiancé helped me to see how this experience was for him. He felt slimed. I had taken on Angie's stress, had let it cloud my ability to think clearly, and had responded out of anxiety. I still could have felt compassion for her and perhaps taken the same actions, yet without becoming a whirlwind of anxiety. Just as with Clarice, although I seemingly "helped" the two women, it wasn't helpful for me or for them in the long-term.

Learning not to be hijacked or flooded by another's negative emotions is perhaps a lifelong process. I want to be affected by people's lives. It is good and appropriate to weep, get angry, care deeply, and receive others with love and empathy. Empathy, however, does not mean becoming as stressed or fearful as the other person. According to David Benner in *Care of Souls*, empathy is "the ability to enter into the experience of others, or, better, receive their experience as they share it with you, holding it within you in such a manner as not to confuse it with your own."

> *We are entrusted with people's lives, care for people as best as we can, but do not assume their pain as our own.*
> LAURA VAN DERNOOT LIPSKY

In fact, lack of empathy for another's feelings and needs is one of the signs of codependency. A caregiver may sway to the opposite extreme and become detached from feeling empathy for clients. Being in recovery is being "able to feel compassion for another's feelings and needs," according to Co-Dependents Anonymous. The reality is that "personality types who are attracted to the field of helping are more likely to be highly attuned and to feel empathy toward others, which make them good at their job *and* more vulnerable to developing [compassion fatigue, vicarious trauma] and burnout."

It's natural and expected to be affected by another's emotions. "To suffer with" is the literal definition of *compassion*. There is beauty and goodness in simply being with people in their suffering. I've often heard that what was most beneficial in the midst of someone's pain and grief was for someone to be present. No words were needed, no actions helpful. Judith Herman wrote, "The survivor who is often in terror of being left alone craves the simple presence of a sympathetic person." In the garden of Gethsemane, Jesus pleaded with his disciples to stay awake with him, not to fix or change the situation, but just to be present (Matthew 26:40). Those who try to make the other feel better or to answer unanswerable questions can actually cause more damage than healing.

Jesus also beautifully modeled grieving with people when he found out his friend Lazarus had died, and he wept yet again when he looked upon Jerusalem. Jesus engages with the weight of our emotions, our stressors, and our challenges, even though he knows the resurrected life that is coming.

We're invited to come alongside, to suffer with others, and yet also to learn to be led by God and let Jesus carry the weight (Matthew 11:28). We're invited to entrust this grieving, joyous Jesus with our burdens. As if with a fishing rod, we are to "cast" our burdens on God and to trust that God will sustain us (Psalm 55:22). We're called to enter into life with another, though ultimately we point people to Jesus and not ourselves.

God offers the most complete, sacrificial, self-giving love. Yet even in God's immense, boundless love for us, God pursues us without forcing or fixing us. Likewise we can't force ourselves on others. In our own struggle and compassion for others, we can experience God's love and sustenance as we also entrust that God loves those we accompany and is at work outside of us. God's love is not limited to us and our expression of it.

> *Praise be to the Lord, to God our Savior, who daily bears our burdens.*
> PSALM 68:19 (NIV)

Receiving God's love frees us to love others in a way that serves yet doesn't demand, to be connected and yet not possessive. It equips us to love others and to love ourselves.

Below is the Codependency Self-Assessment link. This tool can help you recognize what codependency is and how it may be playing out in your life. It isn't prescriptive or the final word—nor is its goal to add guilt. Take a deep breath and extend grace to yourself before you examine the questions below and take the test.

REFLECTION QUESTIONS

- How do you feel when someone else isn't doing well?
- In what way might you try to fast-forward someone's healing or change of circumstances so that you feel successful, more at ease, and/or better about yourself?
- Who is the "you" that God loves beyond any role or persona?

EXERCISES

- Take the Codependency Self-Assessment online: reachrecovery.org/program/forms/codependency-survey/.
- Attend a Co-Dependents Anonymous or Al-Anon Anonymous meeting. Post somewhere two of the core Al-Anon statements: (1) we admit we are powerless over others, and (2) we can't control other people.

- Pray through one of the listening prayer exercises: "Moving Beyond Codependency," "The Garden Wall," or "Surrendering Burdens" (see appendix two).
- Create your own creative practice of "entrusting" people and situations to God as a way of maintaining healthy attachments with people and work. See the Trust Bowl exercise in appendix one as an example. Learn more about that in chapter thirteen.
- Consider this poem by Heather Tillery.

> When I learn
> this is not love
> I take back the soft pillow
> of myself
> close the ointment's lid
> and weep
> for the pain of it all. . . .
> I undo so much
> I believed was good
> but was never mine to hold
> and was never loving
> to carry.

RECOMMENDED RESOURCES

Addiction and Grace: Love and Spirituality in the Healing of Addictions by Gerald May

Breathing Under Water: Spirituality and the Twelve Steps by Richard Rohr

Codependent No More by Melody Beattie

Tattoos on the Heart by Gregory Boyle

In the Realm of Hungry Ghosts: Close Encounters with Addiction by Gabor Maté

SIX

NEEDS AND DESIRES

Careful attention to one's inner life is an indispensable prerequisite of caring for the souls of others.

DAVID BENNER

Jack Frost was a pastor and the founder of Shiloh Place Ministries. His pastoral journey began after years of addiction to drugs, alcohol, and pornography. He confessed that his addictions were driven by a fear of failure. Although he was in recovery when he started ministry, the same fears motivated his new work. He wrote,

> After my conversion, I became active in church life and quickly learned that my tendency toward performance operated well in a religious environment. I simply transferred my ungodly beliefs, my fear of failure, and my aggressive striving into church work. I thought that the best way to win God's approval and acceptance was to do things for Him and also to win the favor of the Christians around me.

Unfortunately he was not alone, but was driven by what he calls "hyper-religious activity" alongside his fellow Christians. He confesses believing that "the more we prayed, fasted, read our Bibles, witnessed to strangers, or attended church meetings, the more acceptance we thought we gained from God." Without his awareness, Jack's desire for acceptance from God and fellow Christians drove his newfound ministry workaholism. He had simply replaced one addiction with another.

Laura van Dernoot Lipsky and Connie Burk say that a critical question to continually ask ourselves is "Why am I doing what I'm doing?" It's normal to have mixed motives for being engaged in our work. We might be aware of some of our reasons, such as compassion, love for others, determination to decrease poverty and oppression, personal experiences, family history, and having a strong sense of calling. Nevertheless we might not realize our codependency or how we're seeking to meet other needs and avoid certain fears.

For many of us who are engaged in ministry and helping professions, it seems easier to focus on the needs and characteristics of others rather than our own. We're often focused on asking questions of others, listening, problem solving, or assessing needs. We become out of touch with who we are and our desires, strengths, and brokenness. We stop listening to ourselves and to the wisdom of others. We speed up and go, go, go, overworking and thinking we're doing it all for God.

To move toward health and sustainability, it's beneficial to unpack how we view our needs and how they drive us. We can then explore how to hold caring for our needs in tension with the invitation to self-sacrifice.

NAMING OUR NEEDS

As mentioned previously, throughout my life I've had a hard time acknowledging my needs and desires. For years I believed I shouldn't want or need things for myself. I had a hard time allowing myself to do life-giving activities. I unconsciously thought desire was bad, wrong, and should be denied if I am to be a loving Christian woman. I interpreted the biblical invitation to deny ourselves as "always deny our needs and desires." My self-denial was partly due to my interpretation of Philippians 2:4 (ESV): "Look not to your own interests, but to the interests of others." I thought it meant that I should always put others' needs before my own, so taking time to myself would be selfish because it meant I was "looking to my own interests."

I've come to learn that over-giving is often a sign of deprivation—a signal that a need isn't being met, an emotion isn't being expressed, or a void isn't getting filled.
CHERYL RICHARDSON

Combined with female social conditioning, the Christian invitation toward self-denial meant that others' needs were more important than my own. I considered the needs of many people as valid, so to me theirs didn't signify weakness or selfishness. In contrast, I judged my own needs and desires as evidence of dependency and weakness. As a result, I learned to deny my needs.

What I wanted or needed didn't really matter.

Without knowing it, I was setting the stage for codependent rescuing behavior. My identity became founded on how capable and helpful I was—and not as a beloved daughter. Understanding that our needs are not only important but also part of being human is essential to moving toward wholeness. It's an ongoing journey to learn that having needs doesn't mean I'm weak. I am *human* for having needs.

Some think of needs primarily in terms of food, shelter, and safety. Yet our human need for love and connection is central across disciplines, whether it's Maslow's well-known hierarchy of needs, Contemplative Outreach's fundamental needs, or Judith Herman's distilled list of "safety, satisfaction, and connection—that are grounded in our ancient evolutionary history." What all these approaches agree on is that these needs are normal, healthy, and necessary, and we seek to meet our needs whether we're aware of it or not.

When I don't take lunch breaks, work long days, or check work email on days off, I'm meeting some of my personal needs—not just being "self-sacrificial." Perhaps I am meeting my need to be productive, helpful, or valuable. Subconsciously I believe, *Look how stressful my life is, how hard working I am. I must be important because I work a lot and have so many demands. People must need my help.*

Motivations can often be messy, and examining them can feel raw. Common needs that we might seek to meet in our work—and not necessarily through codependent behavior—include a need for impact, intimacy, approval, identity, and self-worth. Our need to have an impact on the world can lead to dissatisfaction, frustration, and even harm to those we serve. We might develop a martyr complex that projects pride in our work when in reality we feel bitter and self-sacrificial.

Our desire for accolades trumps our capacity to love.

Examining our own needs can clarify whether our frustration or exhaustion is about the person we are working with or about some unmet need in ourselves. Recognizing and naming our needs is a core component of nonviolent communication (NVC), a way of resolving conflict. The creator of NVC, Marshall Rosenberg, describes how judgments and criticisms "of others are all alienated expressions of our needs. . . . Most of us have never been taught to think in terms of needs. We are accustomed to thinking about what's wrong with others when our needs aren't being fulfilled." Our skill at meeting our needs develops early in order for us to cope and survive. We develop patterns of behavior that establish a "program for happiness" and form our false self.

Acknowledging that I'm broken and have needs has been my first step toward liberation. To realize how I have tried to meet those needs in unhealthy ways, thinking I'm actually being unselfish, is humbling and heartbreaking. Referencing the story of the prodigal son, Jack Frost wrote, "As soon as our service is no longer motivated by God's love but by a need to be needed or seen, we begin to drift away from Father's heart of compassion, and we will soon find ourselves in the older brother's shoes, slaving in the fields and thinking that all along we dwell in His house of love." Richard Rohr called this "the myth of heroic sacrifice." He added, "There is a love that sincerely seeks the spiritual good of others, and there is a love that is seeking superiority, admiration, and control for itself, even and most especially by doing 'good' and heroic things."

WELCOMING AND SURRENDERING OUR NEEDS

We are created with needs. Jesus charged his listeners to not worry about their basic needs for clothing, food, and water, explaining that "indeed your heavenly Father knows that you need all these things" (Matthew 6:32). Our practical needs are important to God. We don't need to prove our surrender to God by denying what we need and long for. In doing so, we deny that God is our creator and the dreamer within us.

Often we have to wait for our hopes and longings to be fulfilled. It's hard to stay in the liminal space of waiting for companionship, for community, for finances, for healing, for systemic changes. The fact that our desires are unfulfilled doesn't mean they aren't valued by God or worth hoping for. As the psalmist wrote, God turns his ear toward us to hear what we want and fulfill our needs (Psalm 116:2; 37:4).

Jesus directed people to voice their desires and needs to him, asking, "What do you want me to do for you?" Whether it was the woman pushing her way through the crowds to touch his cloak or the blind man yelling on the side of the road, Jesus saw and welcomed people uniquely, invited them to express what they wanted, and lovingly addressed their concern. Ruth Haley Barton wrote, "Such questions had the power to elicit deep honest reflection in the person to whom they were addressed and opened the way for Christ to lead them into deeper levels of spiritual truth and healing." Jesus often asked questions to open the door for those he helped, not offering suggestions but welcoming people to articulate their need.

Yet clearly all our desires aren't in line with who God is and who we are created to be. Nor is satisfying our desires the ultimate goal. When we take steps toward recovery, it can be tempting to swing to the other extreme: independence. Life becomes about meeting our own needs and not tending to those of others.

The plight of many self-care strategies is that they are utterly self-focused. Western culture often encourages self-preoccupation, touting individualism instead of interdependence as the highest ideal. Many other cultures emphasize interdependence, such as the well-known South African concept of *ubuntu*—in which our humanity is bound up with each other's. It's also illustrated by Chief Sealth's concept of the "web of life." If one piece of the web is unraveling, it affects the whole web—in large and small ways. If I'm stressed and overwhelmed by my work, I carry that into my work and relationships. My unraveling affects not only me but also those around me. As Lipsky mentioned in her class, "What good is it then to be taking care of another piece of unraveling web if our own piece is also falling apart?"

Our desolation affects each other, and so can our consolation. As retired archbishop and anti-apartheid activist Desmond Tutu said, our individual flourishing "should enhance the lives of others, not detract from them. . . . We must care for one another in order to thrive." He said this as one who sacrificed his personal flourishing, persevering in the face of death threats in order to speak out against the institutionalized racism of the apartheid system.

We are urged to seek God's kingdom first, above our desires and personal needs, trusting that God will give us the desires of our heart (Matthew 6:33; Psalm 37:4). We are called toward self-sacrifice and to love others in the same way that Jesus loved us.

And Jesus surrendered his life for us.

For many, speaking truth to power comes at great cost. Civil rights leader and pioneer of Christian Community Development John Perkins was also beaten and harassed due to his activism against racism and injustice. His life and writing demonstrate how putting the needs of others above our own "lays the groundwork for reconciliation to occur." Even still, he offers his humble confession and reflection as he looks back at his life: "I realize that there were times that I allowed fear to prevent me from telling all the hard truth. When others didn't want to hear it I could have been bolder in pressing forward." His fear for his safety was and is valid, as it is for many who pursue justice. Yet he confesses to wishing he had laid aside his concern about what people thought and allowed himself to speak up more, regardless of how uncomfortable it made people feel.

I wonder too if sometimes the self-interest that I should put aside is my need to be accepted and esteemed, to be safe and comfortable. My desire to please others has kept me from speaking the truth and loving others well. As a result, in addition to being silent in the face of injustice, sometimes I haven't challenged people when they made choices that were detrimental to their well-being. One woman I knew for years was in a relationship that repeatedly dragged her down. She often came to me in tears, expressing her frustration with her partner's substance addiction and its effect on their lives. She'd share her desire to leave her partner. We'd talk through options and make a plan.

But the next week she was madly in love again and wanting to get married—to the same guy. I witnessed this cycle four to five times. Each time it broke my heart. Although I knew I wasn't responsible for her choices and couldn't change her, I didn't challenge her or remind her of the goals she had made. Instead of "looking to her interests" and prioritizing her well-being, my need to be liked, and my desire to retain our connection probably drowned out any timid attempts to help her.

As I reread "Let each of you look not only to your own interests, but also to the interests of others" (Philippians 2:4 ESV), I notice that it isn't saying my interests or needs are bad. It's encouraging us to *also* pay attention to the interests of others. This is very different from saying that our interests or needs aren't important and should be neglected. In healthy relationships, we can be ourselves, stand up for our opinions and beliefs, and not pretend we agree or say yes, just to be liked. Perhaps I say no to someone's request because I don't have the energy and wouldn't be fully present to that person. In doing so I'm actually putting that person's interests before my own need to be liked. I know that I'll be more present and centered when we do get together, honoring them and their time.

Love is patient. It does not rush. It does not fix. It gives space for the Spirit to heal and restore. It moves us as close as we can get to the pain and suffering of our brothers and sisters. . . . We belong by recognizing that when one part of the body hurts, we all hurt.

REESHEDA GRAHAM-WASHINGTON AND SHAWN CASSELBERRY

As followers of Jesus, we're invited to know and experience a belovedness that doesn't depend on how others perceive us. Consider the apostle Paul's questions: "Am I now seeking human approval, or God's approval? Or am I trying to please people? If I were still pleasing people, I would not be a servant of Christ" (Galatians 1:10). Christ equips us to love from an honest, authentic place. As we allow the Spirit to move within us, to heal and restore us, we're transformed more into Christ's likeness. Our desires are transformed, and we are free to participate more fully with God in loving those around us. We're able to recognize what is ours to bear and what unmet needs are driving our behavior. We're also more aware of our true self's needs and desires, the desires that God wants to meet in full.

Jesus invites us to surrender our needs to him, to speak the truth even if we aren't heard, and to voice our needs even if it inconveniences another—and ourselves. Self-giving love is not self-serving love. We're invited to express a sacrificial love of others, a love that requires our energy, compassion, and the denial of our interests. However, we're also invited to a love for ourselves that incorporates addressing our own needs. We hold onto the truth of God's delight in us as we pursue God's kingdom and receive God's nourishment. God wants to journey with us and satisfy our thirst in our most parched and broken places.

We become vessels of and for shalom. We continue our journey, moving *from* belovedness not *for* belovedness. In chapter nine, we'll explore the Welcoming Prayer practice as a contemplative way of offering our needs to God.

Marshall Rosenberg's *Nonviolent Communication* book and online inventory lists about forty basic human needs, summarized into seven categories: autonomy, celebration, integrity, interdependence, physical nurturance, play, and spiritual communion.

To begin exploring your needs and desires, take a look at these core universal human needs and reflect or free-write on the following questions.

REFLECTION QUESTIONS

- What do you need to feel cared for and to care for yourself?
- What personal needs are you seeking to meet in your work? In what ways are you serving out of guilt? Or working to fulfill the hopes and expectations of your community? Or responding out of the need to be needed or have value?
- What does your piece of the web look like, and how does it affect those around you?
- In what ways do you seek approval from others? What would it look like to seek approval from God and not through your work? How does your desire for approval affect your willingness to speak out?

EXERCISES

- Explore the "Nonviolent Communication Needs Inventory," cnvc.org/Training/needs-inventory.
- Consider the poem *The Blessings of Jesus* by John Philip Newell (poetic rendition of Matthew 5:3-9 at heartbeatjourney.org/casa-del-sol-blessing-of-jesus/).

RECOMMENDED RESOURCES

Nonviolent Communication by Marshall Rosenberg
Experiencing Father's Embrace by Jack Frost
Life Together by Dietrich Bonhoeffer

SEVEN

FALSE BELIEFS

It's not so much the things that happen to us that still affect us. It is the distorted belief systems or lies that were produced from the trauma that are still controlling our thoughts, emotions, and behaviors.

MICHAEL DYE, *GENESIS PROCESS* COUNSELORS MANUAL

Many social workers and therapists have expressed to me that they know they "should" take better care of themselves. They know what is life-giving to them, and what changes they want to make in their own lives. They're aware of their needs and desires. Yet they repeatedly run themselves dry, neglect priorities, and avoid taking breaks. They make plans to change their behavior because of exhaustion and signs of burnout; yet without addressing the roots, the cycle is repeated.

One barrier to taking care of ourselves is that we don't feel worthy of care. "Not feeling worthy" is a belief or narrative we have about who we are. Society assigns people different worth. We thrive best when we know we're loved regardless of what we do or how society treats us. This is living out of our belovedness.

In reality, we may have limited time for rest and refreshment. Yet if we don't believe we're valuable when we rest, then sufficient time isn't the true barrier. We have to believe we deserve and need care to practice self-care. Without this foundation, seeking to change our behavior will be futile.

To further understand why I raced through my days and didn't stop to take a lunch break or even go the bathroom, I needed to unpack the beliefs behind those actions.

THE TIE BETWEEN BELIEFS, EMOTIONS, AND BEHAVIORS

The fact that our beliefs create emotions, which drive our behaviors, is one of the core tenets of the Genesis Process, a relapse prevention program. It's based in biblical and neurochemical frameworks and utilizes various psychological and inner-healing tools to understand "what is broken that causes us to be self-destructive."

When one is a stranger to oneself then one is estranged from others too. If one is out of touch with oneself, then one cannot touch others.
ANNE MORROW LINDBERGH

Our beliefs about ourselves, our worth, and our purpose drive our attempts to meet the needs that motivate our work. I shared earlier that I believed I had tapped out my care supply, as if there is such a thing. Comparison is a beast that can lead to misguided motivations and false conclusions that end in shame. I started believing I didn't need (and shouldn't need) help, which was both untrue and prideful.

Beneath my false belief was also a false identity rooted in shame. I've often felt shame for being American and European American. Added to that, I've felt shame for being white. Whiteness became "a symbol only of injustice, undeserved privilege and the evil of racism," as Brenda Salter McNeil and Rick Richardson poignantly shed light on in their book *The Heart of Racial Justice.* I developed what they call a "hip white person identity . . . the attempt of European American people to become or be identified as 'black' or 'hispanic,' usually out of shame or guilt about their own culture. . . . Their sense of worth is based on the acceptance they receive from the particular group they are trying to identify with." I can't count the number of times while I was in Central America or with Mexican families in the United States that people have asked me where I'm from after hearing me speak Spanish. I have said "de Cuba" or "de Argentina." I've longed to belong with people I love and admire—and I've not wanted to belong to America or to be white.

White guilt is especially toxic when combined with a messiah complex—another false identity. As described by Ryan Kuja in a 2019 *Sojourners* article, "6 Harmful Consequences of the White Savior Complex," the White Savior Complex is present when "experts swoop in with their answers and expertise and fail to include the voices of local leaders, organizations, and stakeholders." White people think they know the answers about how to be God's hands and feet in the world, so they seek to help "those" people who need it. In doing so, they perpetuate the belief that white people don't need help. I wonder if I often subconsciously approached people as "helpless" and myself as the heroic helper. The White Savior Complex "makes us into heroes rather than empowering others to become the heroes of their own stories." It feels powerful to be the one helping others.

False beliefs influence our feelings of anger, shame, resentment, and guilt. When they provide the narrative we live by, we're more triggered by our own or others' emotions and less able to care well for the person in front of us. This may lead us down a path toward codependency instead of a love born out of freedom. For example, when we believe our identity is based on what we do or on a rejection of who we are, those we try to help become projects that our success depends on. Their failure is thus our failure. Our work becomes driven by our need to feel successful, not by our desire to improve another's well-being. Then, as Nouwen put it, "we not only have successes, we become our successes."

When I live that way, the remedy to failing is for me to try harder and do more. I begin wanting someone else's change more than they do. I move ahead with my agenda for their lives, not realizing they are potentially ashamed of saying no or disappointing me. This develops into a need to control another's life and alienates me from the very people I am trying to help.

Changing our false beliefs is crucial for moving toward recovery, resilience, and wholeness. If we don't unpack our false beliefs, we will stay in the same cycles and relapse into old behavior patterns. According to the Genesis Process, "A person's self-destructive behavior is the expression of their beliefs, so along with focusing on changing behaviors, Genesis also concentrates on identifying and changing the faulty belief systems that drive self-destructive behaviors."

As I mentioned previously, I've needed to slow down and consider what my identity is based on. When I value only what I do, rather than who I am, I work feverishly. But when I hear from God how truly, deeply loved I am, no matter what I do, I'm free to receive and to give out of fullness. By making small changes, such as turning off my phone, taking a lunch break, and protecting times of rest, I'm heeding the voice of the Beloved. That voice says my value is not in what I do; I deserve care, have limits, and am not superwoman.

IDENTIFYING FALSE BELIEFS

False beliefs can come from messages we received when we were younger. They may be something we've told ourselves to survive or cope with a traumatic situation or reality. Dan Allender, trauma therapist and author of *The Wounded Heart,* points out that for someone who's experienced abuse, it is not uncommon to conclude that "trust is foolish." Yet despite their utility, false beliefs are sometimes referred to as ungodly beliefs because they don't represent the truth of how God sees us or who we are called to be in this world. An inner-healing prayer ministry, Restoring the Foundations, identifies the impact of our childhood environment on developing our beliefs:

> From the moment we enter this world, bits and pieces of information and impressions continue to come together to form our beliefs and expectations. We consciously or unconsciously form opinions and make conclusions. Often these opinions and conclusions are wrong. . . . These ungodly beliefs, developed over time, often seem reasonable to us based upon the facts and experiences of our life.

Present-day experiences and circumstances also impact our beliefs. McNeil and Richardson wrote, "Every day we all—consciously or unconsciously—receive false messages that attempt to define us and tell us who we are. As these messages penetrate our heart, we develop a false self-identity that influences how we view others and ourselves." In addition to writing about white superiority and the hip white identity, McNeil and Richardson describe how people of color may develop false identities to survive repeated exposure to oppression and injustice. These false identities may be based on self-hatred, rage, being the victim, or being the model minority. If you have a model-minority identity, you "may see it as your responsibility to be a positive role model for your entire racial or ethnic group or to dispel negative stereotypes about your people by performing at high levels." A person may generate the belief that "it's all up to me" or "my reputation is on the line, and shame would feel like death."

Here are other examples of common false beliefs.

- If I perform well enough, I can change things.
- If I let go of control, something bad will happen.
- If something's wrong or someone is treating me poorly—even abusively—it's my fault.
- Others' feelings are more important than mine.
- Nothing good comes from conflict. False peace is better than no peace.
- I was created to help others. Because I can help, I should help.
- I have value only when I'm needed.
- My needs are secondary to those of others.
- If I say no, I'll be rejected, let someone down, or worse.

Recognizing our false beliefs is the first step. As McNeil and Richardson wrote, "We must admit that we have rejected ourselves and our ethnic background." In order to unpack some of your beliefs that drive your emotions and behaviors, spend some time with the reflection questions below.

> *To be wholesome, we must remain truthful to our vulnerable complexity.*
> JOHN O'DONOHUE

It can be overwhelming to unpack our false beliefs and false identities. That's why we undergo a recovery *process* and a *journey* of soul care. We also aren't meant to journey alone. Change takes time and requires support, as we will explore in the following chapters. Sometimes we experience significant turning points, revelations and inner healing, and yet it is largely a life-long journey of small steps toward change.

As I have developed a stronger identity in being loved for who I am, my sense of worth is not shaken as easily. But I still resist acknowledging my needs and asking for help. What does it look like to honor how God has made me and yet not base my identity on being a helper? I'm created to be alive, to exercise my gifts, and to live into my true self. I need to continue to counter the false narratives that my value depends on my identity as a helper and that I shouldn't receive support. Living from those narratives is neither honoring of others nor true to myself.

In the chapters ahead, we'll continue to explore the impact of our beliefs. We'll also dive into inner healing and relapse-prevention tools for changing our beliefs and, subsequently, our behavior.

REFLECTION QUESTIONS

- What are some of the reasons you don't take care of yourself? What keeps you from taking time off?
- In what ways do you live as though your worth is based on what you do or how others perceive you?
- What beliefs underlie your need for success and your need for approval?
- How do your family history, ethnic and racial identity, social location, and gender identity impact your sense of worth and beliefs about yourself?

EXERCISES

- Identify one or two primary false beliefs that impact your ability to take care of yourself.
- Explore the Scripture references and prayer exercise, "Replacing False Beliefs" found in appendix two. (Chapter eleven explores how we can change our beliefs in more depth.)
- Find out if there is an available counselor trained in the Genesis Process to take you through the individual counseling manual.

Bring these false beliefs to that counselor, or a therapist, spiritual director, or pastor.

RECOMMENDED RESOURCES

The Heart of Racial Justice: How Soul Change Leads to Social Change by Brenda Salter McNeil and Rick Richardson

Restoring the Foundations, restoringthefoundations.org

The Genesis Process, genesisprocess.org

PART THREE

RECOVERING

The immanent God in us becomes wounded with us, suffers, struggles, hopes, and creates with us, shares every drop of our anger and sadness and joy. . . . We should not be dismayed that God's being surpasses understanding, for it is precisely through this mystery that God incarnate can both share our condition and powerfully deliver us from it.

GERALD MAY, ADDICTION AND GRACE

EIGHT

IDENTIFYING STAGES OF CHANGE

Not everything that is faced can be changed, but nothing can be changed until it is faced.

JAMES BALDWIN

My recovery journey hasn't been a straight trajectory from burnout toward healing. I doubt it ever is for anyone. At times I've wondered if I'll ever change, if I'll ever stop living out of my need to be needed or my need for affirmation and approval. I think I've moved beyond an area of struggle, only for it to show up again a week later, sometimes months or years later. In my journals from nine years ago I came across the same barriers I've been struggling with recently. At first I felt despair, thinking, *Have I not changed? Have I not made any progress?* Instead, I wonder if my journey is like a labyrinth: each time I circle around, I'm moving deeper toward transformation.

I'm learning to give myself permission to rest, to get away, and to be nourished by solitude and time with God. Recently, while on an Ignatian silent retreat, I felt drawn to walk through a labyrinth, acknowledging and asking forgiveness for the fears and false beliefs I continue to struggle with. As I stood in the middle of the labyrinth, I noticed that when I looked back to the beginning, it looked almost like a straight path to the exit. It would have been easy to ignore the curve that would take me back through the maze. I wanted to walk straight out, skip the twists and turns, be done with the same struggles and live in my belovedness. I want repentance to mean that I am changed and won't return to my old ways. I want to have it all together—and then I realize, that in itself is a return to one of my false beliefs.

Instead, the way back involves returning through the maze. Sometimes it feels like I'm going the wrong way, and I don't know when I'll get out. It reminds me to *practice* living as beloved and walking toward new beliefs and behaviors.

One layer into the maze, it seemed I was still at the center. Yet in reality I was one layer farther along. So it is with our barriers; we might struggle with some of the same false beliefs and fears throughout our lives, yet in reality we're going deeper, we're growing stronger.

At times, we may experience rapid change and inner healing, but more often we grow through incremental change. We extend grace to ourselves day by day as new layers are revealed. We forget, make mistakes, and even relapse into old behavior. All of this is part of recovery.

There are a variety of ways to conceptualize how we change our behavior. Let's explore three: the Transtheoretical Model, which outlines common stages in behavior change; the FASTER Scale, which considers the factors that lead to relapse and recovery; and the Journey Model, which describes growth and challenges for followers of Jesus. These models can be used to recognize how ready we are to change our behavior, what triggers us, and what the recovery journey involves.

TRANSTHEORETICAL MODEL: STAGES OF CHANGE

My friends and former colleagues Danielle and Kevin Riley, who are in recovery from substance addictions, were willing to share a bit their recovery journey. Danielle became clean during her first stay in jail, and she left jail not planning on using drugs, however, according to her:

> Circumstances placed drugs literally in my hands within a week of release. The thought of not using didn't have a chance to manifest in my mind before I was high. I had no plan, I had no sober community, and nothing was healed in me. The next attempt at recovery was due to another stay in jail. This time I was pregnant and committed to making it work. The biggest obstacle I encountered was coming to terms with my weakness in my addiction. I couldn't trust myself: my thoughts or reasoning. At every weak moment, my mind was whispering reasons and excuses to use drugs.

Like many who pursue recovery, Danielle experienced a spiral of changing behavior. We might want to change, but we don't have a viable plan. When we're triggered, it's easy to relapse. We try again, this time more aware of the barriers and with renewed strength to face them.

The Transtheoretical Model, developed by Prochaska and DiClemente, involves a Stages of Change tool that is often utilized in social work and counseling. It helps assess an individual's readiness to change their behavior—recognizing that we're all on a spectrum of awareness and desire to change. We need to acknowledge we have a problem before we're able to take steps toward change.

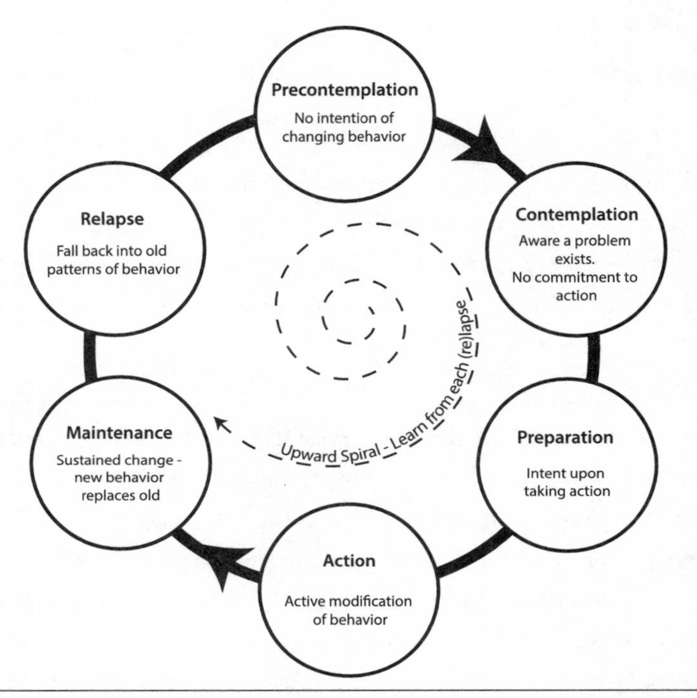

Fig. 8.1. Stages of Change diagram. © Psychology Tools. Reprinted with permission.

Applying this model to *trauma-informed soul care* might look like this:

- ***Precontemplation.*** We aren't aware we have a problem or that we are nearing burnout. We think we're fine, that self-care is for others.
- ***Contemplation.*** We're aware we aren't doing well but have no plans to change anything. We're just beginning to think about some reasons to change.
- ***Preparation.*** We recognize that we have a problem and need to change. We start to think through what changes we can make. We might start asking for help.
- ***Action.*** We make a few small steps toward change. Perhaps we integrate one daily practice into our lives. For example, instead

of checking email immediately upon waking, we wait until after we've centered for the day through prayer and meditation.

- ***Maintenance.*** We continue with this new behavior, avoiding the old behavior of checking email right away. We sustain this change for a few weeks.
- ***Relapse***. We convince ourselves the old behavior isn't a big deal or that we'll just do it this once. The next morning we do the same, and before we know it, we've replaced our new behavior with the old.

This cycle continues as we move toward health. The Stages of Change incorporates the reality of relapse, which we will explore next. However, it doesn't include the potential return to a previous stage before moving forward and assumes that one is always making thoughtful, coherent, and logical choices. Changing our behavior does not involve a nice straight line, it is more like the labyrinth, with twist and turns. In order to get out of the cycle, we need to recognize what patterns lead to relapse. We turn the corner of the labyrinth and gain new perspective.

THE FASTER SCALE

Most people relapse to their previous addiction at least once. In fact, when asked, "Does relapse to drug abuse mean treatment has failed?" The National Institute for Drug Abuse states, "No. The chronic nature of the disease means that relapsing to drug abuse at some point is not only possible, but likely." Danielle's husband, Kevin, said,

> The whole first year of recovery is vulnerable . . . actually the first couple of years. PAWS [Post-Acute Withdrawal Symptoms] is real. You can be stone cold sober and suddenly go through the feelings of being high again. If not handled

> correctly, it is easy to relapse. For all the damage that it does to you, getting wasted is the most beautiful thing in your mind. Using substance is a way out.

Danielle added, "When you have found your drug of choice, relapse is so common because it is the drug that works best to alleviate any feelings of distress, shame, or depression."

I encountered many women in jail who relapsed after years of sobriety because of the death of a close friend or a family member. They didn't have healthy tools to cope with the painful emotions that rushed to the surface. Using drugs and alcohol had been their strategy to numb feeling. For this reason, Michael Dye, creator of the FASTER scale, calls addictions "anesthetics." According to him, "Knowing what to do when this occurs is a critical skill in relapse prevention."

Because biological and physiological changes can clue people in to a potential to relapse, Dye created the FASTER Scale to help those in recovery identify the behaviors and circumstances that contribute to staying in recovery and relapsing. FASTER is an acronym for the steps toward relapse: Forgetting priorities, Anxiety, Speeding up, Ticked off, Exhausted, Relapse. Identifying the predominant behaviors in each of the sections reveals potential triggers that serve as red flags for an individual and their support network.

Sensing, naming, and identifying what is going on inside is the first step to recovery.
BESSEL VAN DER KOLK

The FASTER Scale also acknowledges the "dry relapses" that happen before someone actually uses a substance. Negative emotions are often channeled into anger and anxiety to block pain. Kevin doesn't relapse with a substance anymore, but with anger. "I previously used drugs and alcohol so I didn't have to feel anything and could shut people down with it. Anger was always a byproduct of my drug use. I'd get angry, strung out, then go beat people up. Or I'd fall into a spiral of lack of self-worth, and use anger to run people off because I didn't feel worthy of their attention." By recognizing his triggers prior to using anger to deal with pain, he is learning to slow down, ask for help, and prevent spiraling into old behavior.

To move toward recovery, it was helpful for me to step out of the labyrinth and to identify my FASTER Scale triggers. I needed to name the priorities I was forgetting or dismissing—primarily time to recenter myself and rest in God. I needed to ask for help and to involve people in my recovery. I needed to recognize how my anxiety was leading me toward "codependent rescuing"—one of the symptoms on the scale. I knew I had a hard time slowing down and saying no, but I hadn't recognized how I was avoiding grief, inadequacy, regret, and guilt. I'd get really busy or I'd speed up both in activity and mindset. Then I'd be upset—at myself for not being strong enough or at others for not supporting me. I'd feel alone yet act as if I didn't need help. Exhaustion hit, and eventually I burned out.

The FASTER Scale helped me to name my addiction to codependent workaholism and to admit I had a problem. It was humbling and heartbreaking to recognize my pattern. Although I've journeyed now a few times around the labyrinth spiral, my triggers are the same. I still need to remember my priorities, slow down, and ask for help before I get exhausted.

Instead of letting relapse spiral us into shame, we can be aware of this reality and our triggers. We can choose to extend grace to ourselves when we mess up and to muster the courage to continue.

THE JOURNEY MODEL

We all know that hurdles don't simply disappear with an initial faith conversion. Nor is life simply about our own recovery. We're invited to grow in wholeness and to offer our lives to others.

Dr. Bruce Demarest offers the Integrated Contemporary Journey Model, adapted from the work of Janet Hagberg and Robert Guelich. It describes the stages of change typically experienced by people of faith as they grow and navigate life's challenges. The model begins with the Converted Life, followed by the Discipled Life, and then the Productive Life. In the third stage, people get busy or "sped-up," similar to the third stage of the FASTER Scale. They may have received "the false message that busyness and accomplishments endear them to God." They overextend themselves and become angry with others and with God. In this stage, it's easy to recognize trauma exposure responses and patterns that lead to burnout. According to Demarest, "Often in this third stage believers may experience a major crisis—a wrenching, face-to-face encounter with their own inadequacy. . . . [Some] throw in the towel. But those who genuinely reexamine their relationships with God use the crisis to catch the vision of a new beginning."

This crisis catalyzes the Inward Journey, the fourth stage. Demarest says, "Persuaded that the old pattern does not work, believers enter deeply with the soul to engage God." They start identifying their priorities and entering again into the Preparation and Action stages of change.

Danielle said she was able to maintain recovery behaviors through asking Jesus to free her from "very frequent thoughts, vivid dreams, and physical urges to use. After a while, Jesus removed them, little by little." She added, "Now, after five years clean and sober, I experience a rare dream but no longer do my thoughts and body yearn for the drugs that held me captive." Danielle and Kevin have both gone through the nearly year-long Genesis Relapse Prevention Counseling program—twice. They continue to do the hard work of recovery, recognizing that underneath substance use are other addictions and fears that they want to be free from.

The Inward Journey describes the soul work we're exploring throughout this book. It's a journey toward connecting with God, oneself, and others; recognizing the need for help, healing, and recovery; and developing new rhythms of rest and networks of support.

However, according to the Journey Model, growth doesn't stop there. The Inward Journey equips people to enter the fifth stage, the Outward Journey. According to Demarest, "God directs those who have made the renewing inward journey back outward into the active world with clear vision and purpose. The call may be to the same ministry, but the motivation is radically different." They reengage with their life and calling in a new way, motivated not to serve their need to be needed but to serve others holistically from a grounded place. This purified outward love leads to the sixth stage, the Journey of Love, in which they surrender their need for approval, for success, and for impact. They seek God's kingdom first, pursuing the priorities God calls them to. They serve others out of an abundance of God's love.

> *The more we heal our own pain, the more we can turn toward others. . . . The more we can turn toward others, the more joy we experience, and the more joy we experience, the more we can bring joy to others.*
>
> **DOUGLAS ABRAMS, ARCHBISHOP DESMOND TUTU, AND THE DALAI LAMA**

Danielle and Kevin Riley exemplify this movement beyond recovery to engage in loving others who are struggling with addiction. They not only tenaciously pursue recovery but also are on staff at Tierra Nueva. Kevin currently pastors a small rural church in a community that has been ravaged by addiction and poverty, and Danielle is pursuing training to be a commissioned pastor. They're incredible advocates for people in recovery and have started a podcast to share about their work.

The Journey Model provides a more expanded vision of health and wholeness than the other models. In it we're invited to be grounded and to reengage in our work and life in a new way. The Outward Journey demonstrates that what has been our greatest burden can become our greatest gift. We are wounded healers.

We also learn and receive from those who've journeyed before us and understand our struggles. It's common for survivors of domestic violence to want to volunteer or work with those who are still stuck in abusive relationships. Alcoholics Anonymous incorporates this desire into its twelfth step. People in recovery are invited to help others struggling with the same addiction, through sharing their stories and becoming sponsors or peer counselors.

Sometimes people want to jump in and help early on in their recovery, bypassing the hard work of the journey inward. This often leads to a relapse. Although our healing can come through accompanying others, we need to be moving through the work of the Inward Journey.

All stages of recovery flow back and forth with dynamism and nuance. For me, offering soul care for others is a movement toward the Outward Journey. Regardless, I continually experience my need for growth and healing.

In the rest of this section, we'll dig deeper into a few tools from addiction recovery programs that are particularly applicable to holistic, trauma-informed soul care: building support, moving from shame to self-empathy, and changing our false beliefs.

REFLECTION QUESTIONS

- According to the various models for stages of change, what is your level of readiness to address your workaholic, codependent behavior?
- Remind yourself of a few goals you've set as you've been reading this book. If you haven't yet made any explicit goals, take some

time to do that now. Otherwise, have any goals lapsed? What are you telling yourself now about those goals? In what ways can you have grace for yourself as you continue this process of change? How will you handle relapsing to previous behavior?

EXERCISES

- Walk through a prayer labyrinth. Find one at labyrinthlocator .com.
- Download the FASTER Scale and explore it in more depth, individually or with a Genesis-trained Counselor, genesisprocess .org/handouts/.

RECOMMENDED RESOURCES

Soul Guide: Following Jesus as Spiritual Director by Bruce Demarest
Free on the Inside: Finding God Behind Bars by Sister Greta Ronningen

NINE

MOVING FROM SHAME TO SELF-EMPATHY

The most dangerous stories we make up are the narratives that diminish our inherent worthiness. We must reclaim the truth about our lovability, divinity, and creativity.

BRENÉ BROWN, *RISING STRONG*

Perhaps you're feeling ashamed after reading the last couple of chapters, understanding your relapse patterns, or doing the codependency self-assessment. Shame isn't the goal of this section or this book. Shame simultaneously undermines our work and drives us toward more frenzied work.

We often jump from guilt to shame, or we confuse the two. Appropriate guilt reveals we *made* a mistake. Shame tells us we *are* a mistake. In Brené Brown's book on leadership, she writes, "Shame is the feeling that washes over us and makes us feel so flawed that we question whether we're worthy of love, belonging, and connection." As we've been exploring, the belief that "I am unworthy" is one of the significant blocks to taking care of ourselves and living out of our belovedness.

Sometimes we are even ashamed *that* we feel anxious or fearful. We forget that change takes time. We get upset when we continue the same behavior, often not noticing our growth and that our growth is spiraling, going deeper into our true selves. Again, growth often involves relapsing and making mistakes.

Shame turns relapse into a spiral downward instead of a journey inward and upward. The Genesis Process Counselors Manual states, "Shame is one of the most powerful, bad emotions, and the limbic system will try to avoid it at all cost." The fear of success and failure can lead to relapsing—all because of shame. This is largely because of the belief that "if I become successful I will eventually fail, hurting myself and others." Shame makes it hard to hope for change.

Shame also keeps us in the mud longer. When a child falls down, if the caregiver reacts with shock and fear, the child will mirror that and start crying. If instead the caregiver responds calmly and gently encourages the child to get up, the child shows resilience, gets up, and brushes off the fall. The internal voices of fear and shame pin us down to the ground, making it harder to brush off our mistakes.

> *When you feel like you have no value, you treat yourself like you don't.*
> SISTER GRETA RONNINGEN

ASKING FOR CLARIFICATION

In relationships with others, often what we fear or hear is not based in truth. If we're stuck in the mud of shame, that mud can clog our ears and make it difficult to hear what someone is really saying. This happens all the time without us realizing it. When we start to experience shame because of what someone else has said or done, it's helpful to ask questions like these: What is the person really saying to me? Is he rejecting me? Is she saying something that's completely different from what I'm hearing?

After my sabbatical and a year working as a youth residential program manager in Seattle, I returned to work at Tierra Nueva. Stemming from my false beliefs, I had a small, unconscious fear that I wouldn't be welcomed back. I notified the directors that I was considering it but hadn't decided. My former supervisor called me to talk. In the course of the conversation, he began telling me how things had changed in the organization. With the mud of shame in my ears, I heard that he thought I wasn't a good fit anymore; I shouldn't come back, I no longer belonged.

My husband overheard snippets of my side of the conversation and saw my face fall. Knowing me, and knowing what might be going on in me, he gave me an encouraging look. I took a deep breath and asked a quick check-in question with my former supervisor, still on the phone: "Are you saying that because of these changes I might not be a good fit?" He affirmed that was far from the truth. He was excited about the changes and had just wanted to share them with me.

Sometimes we need help hearing the truth, and it's important to ask for clarification. We might ask, "So, I'm hearing XYZ. Is that what you're saying?" This gives the other person an opportunity to correct or confirm. It also exposes the self-generated lies so we can understand what others are truly saying. Sometimes just speaking something out loud gives us an opportunity to notice that it is a lie. We can practice small steps of grace, if only little by little.

The mud of shame is not the final story.

DEVELOPING HOLISTIC EMOTIONAL INTELLIGENCE

Emotional intelligence is "the capacity to be aware of, control and express one's emotions, and to handle interpersonal relationships judiciously and empathetically." It has increasingly become a topic of interest, noted by psychologists, contemplative prayer leaders, educators, leadership professionals, and others. This interest reveals that it can be challenging, and important, to identify what we are feeling, as well as the impact our emotions are having on our decisions and behaviors. We feel anxious, which doesn't feel good, so we shove the feeling by using a variety of coping mechanisms. We get busier, work more, eat more, drink more, exercise more.

Holistic emotional intelligence invites surrender and dialogue with God. Instead of rejecting or denying our anxiety, grief, and shame, the path toward freedom is to let ourselves feel, accept, and release our emotions. Clearly this is easier said than done. Western Christianity often rushes to victory and avoids lament. Civil rights leader John Perkins wrote, "We neglect the need within our souls to cry out. It is much easier to ignore the aching in our souls." In his encouragement for the church to embrace the spiritual practice of lament, he pointed out how "psalmists came to God with pure, raw emotion. . . . [God] wants us to empty our hearts of this heaviness." Although much more can be and has been said about developing a practice of lament, it begins with an increasing sense of safety to feel emotions.

As we looked at in chapter eight, many addictions are driven by the desire to avoid negative emotions. Exploring our emotions can be scary, especially if that's uncharted territory. Judith Herman emphasizes establishing safety as the first step toward recovery. Even though jail isn't exactly the safest place, sometimes the space away from outside relationships and/or addictive substances allows things to come to the surface. I witnessed many women begin to face and grieve their countless losses, and painfully learn to handle their emotions in new ways.

What follows is a holistic approach to navigating emotions, called Welcoming Prayer, that was developed by one of Contemplative Outreach's founders, Mary Mrozowski. It can be used in response to experiencing any strong emotion: those that feel negative, such as overwhelmed, frustrated, burdened, resentful, angry, or anxious; or positive, such as thankfulness, joy, or fulfillment. According to Contemplative Outreach, "The Welcoming Prayer is a method of consenting to God's presence and action in our physical and emotional reactions to events and situations in daily life." I've integrated it with additional insight from trauma psychiatrist Bessel van der Kolk and Brené Brown's shame research.

Although I've been attempting to identify my emotions and practice self-empathy for a while, I'm just beginning to incorporate Welcoming Prayer into my life. It has been like tapping into a wellspring of water as I welcome the Living Water to work within me and receive my emotions. I invite you to learn from the work and wisdom of Contemplative Outreach and my spiritual director Lorie Martin, who has contributed to explaining the Welcoming Prayer practice throughout this exercise. Together with these skilled practitioners, we invite the Holy Spirit to guide us.

WELCOMING PRAYER: AN EMOTIONAL-AWARENESS PRACTICE

1. Notice and allow your feelings. Pause, breathe, and invite the Holy Spirit. With love and curiosity, begin to notice what you are feeling and allow yourself to feel it. Contemplative Outreach guides the practitioner:

> Using your intuitive eye, move gently through the body, scanning for any discomfort, pain, uneasiness, itching, heat, cold, tension, tingling, or other sensations. . . . Rest (stop) there and sink into (experience) it. . . . All feelings, whether perceived as positive or negative, are welcomed. Feelings may intensify, dissolve, or change as we are present to them in the moment. Simply follow their movement.

Becoming aware of what's stirring in us requires slowing down. When I'm moving fast—or in recovery language, sped up—it's very hard to be aware of what I'm feeling and needing. I become disconnected from myself. I am also unaware of how the emotions of others are affecting me. My body might desperately try to communicate that I'm stressed, too busy, and near burnout.

Our body does communicate to us if we listen. Bessel van der Kolk says that if we avoid listening, we're unable to detect what's dangerous, harmful, and "just as bad, what is safe and nourishing." We end up turning to other sources to help us regulate or calm down, such as "medication, drugs like alcohol, constant reassurance, or compulsive compliance with the wishes of others." As codependent workaholics, we return to our need to be needed, to have impact, to please others, or to not fail. It's too easy, as Brené Brown says, "to steamroll right over emotion."

Welcoming Prayer encourages us to notice and to allow our emotion without figuring it out in the moment. Brown echoes the importance of just recognizing *that* we are feeling *something*. However, if you're like me, you often want to know what you're feeling and why. She offers some "Rumbling" questions that are part of the Rising Strong process:

- Why am I being so hard on everyone around me today?
- What's setting me off?
- I can't stop thinking about that conversation at work. Why?
- I'm having a strong emotional reaction. What's going on?

We might consider exploring these questions after engaging in Welcoming Prayer.

2. "Welcome" Consent to God's Presence. After allowing ourselves to feel, the second step of Welcoming Prayer is to consent to God's presence with us in our feeling, emotion, thought, and experience. As Lorie Martin described to me, we let the feeling be an invitation to receive God's love. We aren't welcoming anxiety but rather welcoming God's movement in us as we experience anxiety. This is a key distinction. According to Father Thomas Keating,

> [Welcoming Prayer] embraces painful emotions experienced in the body rather than avoiding them or trying to suppress them. It does not embrace the suffering as such but the presence of the Holy Spirit in the particular pain, whether physical, emotional, or mental. . . . [In] giving the experience over to the Holy Spirit, the false-self system is gradually undermined and the true self liberated.

I want to acknowledge my anxiety, let myself feel it, and receive what it might be communicating. However, I don't want to let anxiety take over me. I want to invite God into my anxiety.

3. Let Go: Release Needs to God. Now that we've let ourselves feel what we feel and welcomed God's presence in us, we can release our desires and needs into God's hands. Contemplative Outreach encourages letting go through saying: "I let go of the desire for safety and security, esteem and affection, and power and control. I embrace this moment as it is."

When we let go of our desires, we aren't saying that they're unimportant or that we don't have a need for security, affection, and control. We also aren't saying that we have no reason to fear and that the circumstances we face are safe and healthy. For a person caught in an abusive relationship, fear is justified. We aren't saying to just get over the fear or let go of the emotion.

EQUIPPED TO EXTEND SELF-EMPATHY

When I notice I'm feeling a negative emotion, I want to jump quickly to *letting go* of that feeling because it doesn't feel good. I want to be rid of it and then to connect with God and experience peace. Yet Welcoming Prayer invites us to notice the emotion and feel it in our bodies, to sit with it, and to welcome God with us. It invites us to not reject, deny, or react from the emotion but to say, "God, I need you. Come be with me in this. It feels awful. Hold me."

In that place of pain—not after—we experience God's loving embrace. Transformation happens there. We experience God in our darkness, in our trembling fear, in our paralyzing anxiety. God isn't afraid or judgmental of negative emotions. Jesus himself said he was "crushed with grief" in the garden of Gethsemane (Mark 14:34, The Passion Translation). Yet he also followed this with letting go of his need for security, affection, and control. In the presence of his Father, he relinquished it all and embraced the moment for what it was.

God showed me His compassion and spoke a divine truth,
I made you, dear, and all I make is perfect.
Please come close, for I Desire you.

ST. TERESA OF AVILA

After we have come aware of God with us, in the muck and mire of our emotions and our lives, we take a deep breath and are able to trust and surrender our normal human needs.

We are able to extend the empathy we often give others. Practicing self-empathy and compassion is common in resilience and self-care work. Marshall Rosenberg calls it "emergency first-aid"; we listen to what's going on in us, being present and attentive to others. This may look like checking in with ourselves: "Oh, look at me, feeling that fear of rejection again. Yet it's okay; it makes sense given the circumstances. It's okay to feel what I feel." The key is to notice gently, with compassion and not judgment.

By inviting God into our inner work, we can receive God's grace and perspective. It isn't just up to us to extend grace, empathy, and love toward ourselves. Without first consenting to God's activity within me, I struggle to offer myself empathy. It feels awkward, or I get frustrated and feel ashamed that I'm so hard on myself, jumping right back into the shame spiral.

Instead we can receive God's love into our pain, hear how God sees and feels about us, and experience God's presence with us. When we connect to the Living Water and extend ourselves grace, shame loosens its grip. We can let go more easily, wash off the mud, and feel the freedom that's available to us.

As we cry out to God, God leans in, hears our cry, sets our feet firmly on solid truth, and gives us a new song of praise (Psalm 40). God breaks into our spiral of shame and lifts us up out of the miry pit. God is an active God, responding to our cries for help and freedom. In Psalm 18, God rescues the psalmist, who feels caught in the spiral of death, perhaps a spiral of shame and addiction. The psalmist, presumably David, calls out to God from a tormented place, "The cords of death encompassed me" (18:4). God powerfully responds, tearing through heaven and earth, lightning and thunder, fire and hailstone. After racing toward earth, he wrote,

> He reached down from on high, he took me;
> he drew me out of mighty waters.
> He delivered me from my strong enemy, . . .
> He brought me out into a broad place;
> he delivered me, because he delighted in me.
> (Psalm 18:16-17, 19)

God reaches down and takes hold of us in our suffering, when we are drowning in sorrow and pain. God delivers us from our enemies and frees us from the liar who leads us to believe false ideas about ourselves. God goes to great length to deliver and restore us—not because of pity but because God delights in us.

Welcoming Prayer is a practice that we can engage with at any moment: while leaving a meeting feeling angry and frustrated, while listening to a person share about their abusive partner, or while driving home, staring blankly into oblivion. In these moments, instead of tuning out, shoving, or running, may we tune in to what we're experiencing with grace and compassion. May we allow our emotions to connect us with God, the tender, loving liberator. By grace we are saved—daily, if not moment by moment.

REFLECTION QUESTIONS

- Journal about what triggers shame for you. How does it feel?
- What are some false beliefs that keep you stuck in the shame spiral?

EXERCISES

- Try the listening prayer exercise "Replacing False Beliefs" in appendix two.
- Practice Welcoming Prayer, moment by moment.
- Read Psalm 18 and notice the great lengths God goes to rescue the one in whom God delights.

RECOMMENDED RESOURCES

Rising Strong by Brené Brown

Open Mind, Open Heart by Thomas Keating

Contemplative Outreach, "Welcoming Prayer Tri-fold," www.contemplativeoutreach.org/welcoming-prayer-method/

TEN

EMBRACING OUR NEED FOR OTHERS

It is in beloved community that we find the endurance to identify the false selves that keep us bound to the brokenness of the world. In community we may strive toward our true self, which is bound up in God's promises of healing and restoration.

REESHEDA GRAHAM-WASHINGTON AND SHAWN CASSELBERRY

"What's the worst that can happen if you're dependent on others?" Lorie asked me during a recent spiritual direction meeting.

"I'll feel weak," I answered.

"So, what's the worst that can happen if you're weak?"

"Maybe I'll be rejected." Even as I said it, I knew in reality that while that fear felt true, it was far from the truth.

As humans, we're wired to care for and to respond to each other's genuine requests and needs. We're made for connection, and connection requires interdependence. Our shame and pride can prevent us from asking for what we need and keep us stuck in isolation. One of the key components to resilience and recovery work is that we can't do it by ourselves.

Jesus himself asked for help and received care. He built a team of friends around him, not just for ministry partners but for friendship and support. He allowed and even defended a woman who washed his feet with her hair. He asked to eat and to stay at people's houses. He sat down at Jacob's well while his disciples went and got food; then he broke societal barriers by asking a Samaritan woman for water. He asked his disciples to stay awake with him, not once but three times. He also expressed his disappointment that they had fallen asleep and weren't there for him. He acknowledged and voiced his thirst. He recognized when he needed time alone and went off to the mountains to pray. Although fully God, Jesus was also fully human, with needs and desires.

Moses, who led God's people out of slavery in Egypt, also demonstrated his need to receive help. In the midst of Moses providing the sole counsel and advice for the entire community's interpersonal disputes, his father-in-law, Jethro, put his foot down. He told him, "What you are doing is not good. . . . You cannot do it alone" (Exodus 18:17-18). Moses was wearing himself out by trying to handle all the people's requests alone and "do good."

In response, Moses acknowledged that it had become too heavy a burden for him to bear alone (Numbers 11:14). He pleaded to God, who in response told Moses to invite seventy of Israel's leaders to the tabernacle: "I will take some of the power of the spirit that is on you and put it on them; they shall bear the burden of the people along with you so that you will not bear it all by yourself" (v. 17). And Moses' role was distributed to *seventy* other people. He had clearly taken on too much, and God responded by divvying up his role to a large team. In order to change, Moses needed those close to him to address what they saw happening.

EXPLORING OUR BARRIERS TO RECEIVING HELP

Michael Dye, addictions counselor and founder of the Genesis Process, wrote, "Pride is the number-one enemy of recovery, because it prevents you from asking for help, which leads to isolation, and isolation leads to relapse." Before I experienced burnout, I believed I burdened others when I talked about my work experiences. I was so accustomed to listening to others, it was hard to share about myself and even harder to ask to be listened to. I didn't have the energy to seek after my own support, even though I longed to be heard and known. Although I worked for a Christian ministry with fifteen to twenty staff members, I hesitated to ask others to pray for me.

The soul needs love as urgently as the body needs air. . . . When we love and allow ourselves to be loved, we begin more and more to inhabit the kingdom of the eternal.

JOHN O'DONOHUE

In the midst of this, I felt Jesus kindly say, "Bethany, who do you think you are that you don't need other people? I've created you with needs and to be interdependent. Draw on those around you. It's okay to ask for help."

Jesus demonstrated his humility by washing the disciples' feet. In doing so, he also inherently asked them to humble themselves and receive. He told the indignant Peter, "If you don't allow me to wash your feet . . . then you will not be able to share life with me" (John 13:8, The Passion Translation). This is the way of the kingdom: to serve and to be served. If we want life with Jesus, we need to consider ourselves not too important, healthy, or righteous to receive.

For those of us in the helping professions, it's often easier to help others than to be helped. We may avoid support because it makes us feel vulnerable, needy, and dependent. Furthermore we may not feel safe, because we've experienced backlash when we've reached out. Cheryl Richardson shares some other reasons people don't ask for help:

- It takes too much energy to explain what I need, so I don't bother.
- I hate being disappointed when people don't follow through.
- I don't want to hear no.

She continues, "What all of these examples have in common is, in fact, control—the desire to avoid conflict or disappointment, or the attempt to manage the perceptions of others by not appearing weak." As we explored in chapter six, Western culture perpetuates self-reliance and independence. Asking for help is perceived as weakness. We make a false distinction between helpers and those who are helped—and we prefer to be the former. Many of us long for community and connection yet fear vulnerability and weakness.

I wonder how this view affects those I work with, people who come in need and pain. Do I think of myself as better than them because I perceive myself as capable and strong? Do people somehow pick up on this? Brené Brown wrote, "When you judge yourself for needing help, you judge those you are helping. When you attach value to giving help, you attach value to needing help. The danger of tying your self-worth to being a helper is feeling shame when you have to ask for help. Offering help is courageous and compassionate, but so is asking for help."

When I view needing help as a sign of weakness, I perpetuate my messiah complex and disempower others. When I understand my own aversion to asking for and receiving help, I can be more empathetic and understanding of those I seek to help. I wonder if some of the challenge for Clarice, who ran from the motel job, was that it was embarrassing to come back to us and to say, "I messed up. I need help."

This is why admitting "We are powerless over our addictions" is the first step in twelve-step programs. We need to begin by confessing our weakness.

FOR RESILIENCE AND RECOVERY

I dragged my feet for years before I reached out to a couple of spiritual directors. Now I've been meeting on and off with two spiritual directors, Lorie Martin and Kathy Crosby. Tierra Nueva's director, Mike Neelley, invited Kathy to offer spiritual direction for staff, realizing the importance of external care after a few of us burned out. Now staff have the opportunity to meet with her monthly.

> *Recovery can take place only within the context of relationships; it cannot occur in isolation. . . . Just as no survivor can recover alone, no therapist can work with trauma alone. . . . The work of recovery requires a secure and reliable support system for the therapist.*
>
> JUDITH HERMAN

Meeting with Kathy was and is not only helpful for me personally but demonstrates a movement toward health in the organization as a whole. It states that staff are worth care and support, and that we need places to process, lament, and receive.

Sometimes work is exactly where we are the most triggered or feel the most isolated. In her article "Let's Get Real About Why Women of Color Are So Tired," Sayu Bhojwani wrote about the challenge white-dominated organizations present to people of color. Her primary form of self-care is spending time with a few other women leaders. "This is not systemic change," she wrote, "but supporting each other is a crucial first step to breaking down those feelings of being underestimated and undervalued."

Personal support is essential for our overall health. It has also been shown as the "most powerful protection against becoming overwhelmed by stress and trauma." According to the Headington Institute, which provides training for people engaged in humanitarian and emergency work, supportive relationships actually "correspond to decreased levels of trauma, increased effectiveness in the workplace, and higher functioning teams." We need spaces to share how we are affected, spaces where we don't feel alone, whether in personal relationships or through professional support, such as consult groups, counseling, and mentoring.

Dependence starts when we are born and lasts until we die. . . . In the middle of our lives, we mistakenly fall prey to the myth that successful people are those that help rather than need, and broken people need rather than help. . . . The truth is that no amount of money, influence, resources, or determination will change our physical, emotional, and spiritual dependence on others.

BRENÉ BROWN

Support is also essential for our own recovery. "Isolation is the most prevalent common denominator in all relapse," according to Michael Dye and his work as an addictions counselor for more than twenty years. He wrote, "A balanced recovery plan is having someone who is a spiritual advisor, recovery sponsor, family member, friend, or counselor to ensure accountability."

Just as Moses needed his father-in-law to expose the change he needed to make, we need others to help us see what we are blind to, to ask us thoughtful questions, to challenge our addictive behavior, and to remind us that we have limits. We can't do this work alone, nor can we move from surviving to thriving alone.

Though I now know that I need spaces to share, it still isn't easy for me. I'm not used to being the one to talk. I'm more comfortable asking questions and hearing about others' struggles than sharing my own. Each time I prepare to meet with my spiritual director, I get nervous. I don't like being vulnerable or talking about myself. Yet after each meeting, I walk away profoundly impacted. It's such a gift to be listened to and cared for. Prioritizing these meetings is part of my journey toward health and away from the false belief that I don't need help.

As we invite people to support us, we're inviting them into the dance of mutuality. We may actually be giving them a gift, empowering them to help and to provide for our needs. What if we normalized the flow of giving and receiving help, instead of judging giving as better? When we ask for help, we're reaching out for intimacy as much as anything. We're acknowledging we have limitations; we are human. There's wisdom in knowing our limits. When we acknowledge and embrace our need for love and connection, we're freed to receive the gifts and help that others offer us.

As you move forward in your journey, take some time to explore your barriers to asking for help. Maybe it hasn't been safe or you've been hurt when you've asked for help. Extend grace to yourself as you consider your reasons and when you notice yourself rejecting neediness, dependency, or other fears. Consider inviting someone to help you identify your beliefs. Perhaps you've thought about going to therapy for years, but you feel you don't have time or money for it. See the resources below to aid your process.

REFLECTION QUESTIONS

- In what ways do you have a hard time asking for help or taking time off?
- What are the beliefs that drive your fear of asking for help? Do you want to have it all together, to always be the helper?
- What outside support do you already have—or don't have but might be helpful (therapy, spiritual direction, meetings,

mentorship, etc.)? What avenue of support do you want to pursue right now?

- What key relationships are mutually beneficial and supportive? Who are people that you could proactively ask to be listeners for you? Or ask for help in other ways?

EXERCISES

- Research to find a therapist, mentor, or spiritual director who is a good fit for you.
- Look for a Genesis Process Change Group near you: genesis process.org/find-a-program.

RECOMMENDED RESOURCES

Anam Cara: A Book of Celtic Wisdom, by John O'Donohue
Spiritual Directors International, sdicompanions.org
The Transforming Center, transformingcenter.org
SoulFormation, soulformation.org
American Association of Christian Counselors, aacc.net

ELEVEN

CHANGING BELIEFS AND BEHAVIORS

Be renewed in the spirit of your minds, and . . . clothe yourselves with the new self, created according to the likeness of God.

EPHESIANS 4:23-24

When I finally articulated the false belief "my value depends on what I do," I knew it wasn't true; but I couldn't just convince myself of the alternative. Living into a new true belief was harder than I expected. Unfortunately, identifying the narratives that drive us doesn't lead to automatic change. I needed to identify the fears that drove my beliefs, receive truth about who I am, and walk in new ways.

Throughout this book, you've been invited to explore your beliefs and the impact of shame, trauma, and addictions. Maybe you're in the contemplation stage now, thinking about some reasons to change. Maybe you've taken some new steps yet are starting to wonder whether people can actually change their ways of thinking—or whether they even have the authority to do so.

Many people think that any thought that comes to mind is permissible, just because it showed up. This would be like saying that anyone is invited into your home to stay the night just because they knocked on the door. While hospitality is an incredible gift, we exercise control and discernment over when and to whom we offer that gift. Similarly, we have both the authority and an invitation to take our thoughts captive, allowing the Spirit to transform our minds into the mind of Christ (2 Corinthians 10:5; 1 Corinthians 2:16). We're invited to put away our former ways of being and to be made new (Ephesians 4:22-24).

There are a variety of therapeutic modalities for changing behavior—providing a synthesis is beyond the scope of this book. Instead, after briefly exploring how our bodies learn and retain information, we'll look at a few recovery and inner-healing tools for changing our beliefs and behaviors. These can be used in conjunction with other methods, individually or with a companion. For many, meeting with a therapist and/or spiritual director is vital. Whatever avenues you are now contemplating, support is crucial to establish as you seek to change your behavior.

RETRAINING OUR BODIES AND BRAINS

In our battle to change our beliefs and behaviors, we often feel caught in a double bind. As Romans 7:15 states, "I do not do what I want, but I do the very thing I hate." We may know what the right thing to do is but at the very same time feel that taking steps toward change is overwhelming and even unfathomable. On the other hand, we might have no idea what the right thing to do is. The layers that cloud our decision are too thick to see through.

Michael Dye explains: "Even though you've discovered false beliefs, uncovered the lies and know a new truth, there is a time lag between what your limbic system believes and what your neocortex has learned. This is called limbic lag, a process that can be anywhere from a couple of months to years, but it will get shorter as you continue to uncover and challenge the false beliefs (lies produced from traumatic experiences) and risk trusting again."

Our implicit memory—what we've learned unconsciously since we were in utero—impacts our actions without our awareness. This includes how to walk and ride a bike, as well as how we form our "perceptions, behaviors, emotions, and bodily experiences." It contributes to the development of narratives we believe about the world and ourselves. Implicit memory explains why, when we experience something traumatic, we don't have an explicit memory—a memory of exact details. But we still unconsciously respond to triggers, such as a sound, a smell, or a location.

In his book *Anatomy of the Soul,* Curt Thompson explored the ways spiritual practices and emotional awareness can actually help rewire our brains and change the way we react. He wrote, "The good news is that you do not have to remain in the morass of your implicit memory, straitjacketed by things you don't know you don't know. Despite the fact that you cannot turn back the clock and change the actual events of your life, you can change your experience of what you remember and so change your memory." Even the simple act of telling our story to a trusted person and having it received with compassion and empathy can help change our implicit memory and, as a result, our responses. Empathy and validation carry power and healing-balm for the deep fears and anxieties that chain us.

In order to change, people need to become aware of their sensations and the way that their bodies interact with the world around them. Physical self-awareness is the first step in releasing the tyranny of the past.

BESSEL VAN DER KOLK

Psychiatrist Bessel van der Kolk's work has helped many understand the ways that our bodies hold and heal from trauma. He wrote, "The bodies of child-abuse victims are tense and defensive until they find a way to relax and feel safe." In order to heal, he helps his patients to notice and describe the feelings in their bodies—when tense and when relaxed. He helps them to become aware of their breath, movements, and any sensations.

RECOGNIZE THE IMPACTS OF BELIEF AND UNDERLYING FEARS

Before seeking to change a belief, sometimes we need help understanding how our beliefs are affecting us—our bodies, minds, emotions, and relations. Select a predominant false belief from chapter seven or your own reflections, and consider the following Genesis Process self-evaluation questions:

How does the false belief affect me?

- ***Physically***. How does it result in stress? How does it affect my body?
- ***Mentally***. What do I tell myself to keep believing it? What is the perceived benefit that I receive from believing this?
- ***Emotionally***. How does this belief make me act and feel? How does it protect me? What can I imagine feeling if I tried giving up or changing the belief?
- ***Spiritually***. How does it affect my relationship with and ability to hear from God?
- ***Socially***. How does it affect my relationship with others? How does it affect the way I act or my responses toward others?

As previously mentioned, beliefs drive our emotions, which drive our behaviors. In order to engage in successful recovery, the Genesis Process emphasizes the importance of acknowledging the fears behind changing our behavior and taking practical steps to resolve the issues that affect those fears.

> All compulsive and self-destructive behavior involves a double bind. A double bind is when you are in a lose/lose situation. Or when the thing you need the most is also the thing you fear the most. For example . . . if I don't ask for help, I will stay stuck and isolated. Staying stuck in the middle of a lose/lose situation produces feelings of anger, frustration, hopelessness, depression, anxiety, and fear. These are the very emotions that coping behaviors anesthetize.

As we just discussed, having support is not only essential to recovery and resilience but also central to how we are made. We want and need connection and intimacy, yet each one of us has been wounded. So we fear being vulnerable, let down, and mistreated. We often believe that we are alone in our woundedness, not recognizing that everyone experiences woundedness in unique ways, *and everyone needs help*. According to Dye, "We need the very thing that has hurt us the most: each other." We want and need help, yet we fear that others will think we are weak and needy. These conflicting needs and fears put us in a double bind.

The Double Bind worksheet can help us to identify the fears or beliefs that keep us from moving forward, to acknowledge their impact, and to outline the support and concrete steps we need to take. It invites us to begin by reflecting on the following questions:

> ***If I do change*** (move toward the problem), "What will happen (consequence) if I change and give up the problem/coping behavior? What is the fearful/bad thing (belief) that will happen? I'll be vulnerable to . . . what?"

> ***If I don't change*** (avoid the problem), "What will happen (consequence) if you stay the same, don't change?" Think: "A year from now, where will I be?"

A DOUBLE-BIND EXAMPLE: NOT TAKING BREAKS

In the previous chapter I mentioned how anxiety can drive our busyness. When we're already feeling anxious, the invitation toward self-care can add more guilt and more of a burden or obligation that we feel we need to fulfill. This guilt and pressure can send us into a spiral of anxiety.

When I worked as a program manager for a youth residential program, I went nonstop from the moment I arrived until the end of the day. Even years after experiencing burnout, taking lunch breaks was a challenge. I'd work through them because I just wanted to get home. I also didn't want to face what I was feeling. I raced through the week and crashed hard in the evenings. Finally Friday would come, and I'd find myself feeling anxious about resting well. It took most of Saturday to slow down, and by Sunday evening I was anxious about going back to work the next day. I was caught in a double bind: I needed to take a lunch break and a day off, yet I also resisted doing so.

If I do change. I have to stay longer at work. I have to face slowing down and having unallocated time, which means thinking about my day and feeling emotions. I won't be able to do everything I need to do in a day. As a result, I might disappoint someone or let myself down. If I let people down, I risk their rejection. If I am rejected, I will feel pain and diminished self-worth.

If I don't change. I will keep getting home exhausted, grumpy, anxious, and less pleasant to be around. It is likely that in a year I will burnout, hate my job, have quit, and/or experience serious stress-related side effects. I might work less effectively, be more forgetful, and be less gracious with coworkers. This will lead to a cycle of guilt and shame that could perpetuate the beliefs that I'm not enough and need to work harder. I'll refuse to take breaks and respond even more poorly to coworkers or people in my personal life.

Clearly change was necessary, and yet challenging to enact. The anxiety in my job was spilling over into my evenings and weekends. It wasn't that I was scared of resting; I was overwhelmed by my job and needed restorative weekends in order to have the clarity and courage to make changes. In a meeting with Lorie, she asked me, "What is the anxiety telling you? It's probably trying to tell you something. It won't go away unless it is listened to." This was before I knew about Welcoming Prayer, and it was an early encouragement to notice and to allow myself to feel instead of shoving away the anxiety.

Lorie encouraged me to take even short breaks during my day—a walk outside, a few deep breaths. As I mentioned in chapter nine, when I'm sped up in overdrive, I'm literally out of touch with what my body is communicating, let alone what others are saying. Deep breathing, walking, and intentionally engaging our senses are ways to slow down and self-regulate, or calm down our flight, fight, and freeze responses.

After slowing down, I could look at what the anxiety was telling me and how my beliefs were affecting me. It didn't take long to realize that the anxiety was screaming: This job is not a good fit! It's completely draining, and it's even contrary to how I want to be in this world.

I began trying to accept my limitations and to give myself permission to not be superwoman—let alone have it all together. But I was still anxious day in and day out. There was something more I couldn't quite put my finger on. In another meeting with Lorie, she invited me to ask Jesus, "What am I afraid of?" Often beneath anxiety is fear. What surfaced was the fear of both letting people down and being crushed by the demands of my job.

For a recovering social-justice workaholic, setting boundaries and admitting that something is "too much" immediately triggers my fear of not being enough: not tough enough, not strong enough. In response I often work harder and try to suck it up. Therapist Aundi Kolber calls this white-knuckling, saying, "We white-knuckle when we: ignore signs of pain, hunger, or exhaustion," we minimize or are overwhelmed by our emotions, or we are driven or defeated by our adrenaline. Healing begins with recognizing our needs and admitting our brokenness. We need to hear truth from the source of truth to truly set us free and counter the voice of the liar, which fuels our sense of shame and false beliefs.

EMBRACING TRUTH

Once we're aware of our false beliefs and ready to embrace truth, we can take them to Jesus, either on our own or through therapy, spiritual direction, and inner healing prayer. Jesus can free us from shame and decrease a false belief's effect and power over us. As we listen to Jesus' loving voice speak truth to our core, we are freer to be who we were created to be. Just like unlearning an old habit and learning a new one, it takes time after receiving prayer and counseling to live into true and godly beliefs about ourselves.

Dr. Brenda Salter McNeil and Rick Richardson speak specifically to the self-hatred we can carry for our ethnic identities. In order to embrace our true selves, we need to admit "that we have rejected ourselves and our ethnic background" and recognize how this rejection has contributed to our false self. We may also need to admit how we have judged others: perhaps those we seek to serve, perhaps those whose policies and protocols impact the lives of those we love.

In the same way, we need to turn away or "repent" from accepting false identities and narratives. We declare them to be false and receive the truth: "We are the good creation of God." We ask for forgiveness and forgive ourselves, as well as our parents, caregivers, community, and even the larger society for speaking contrary messages. Pastor and activist Carlos Rodriguez beautifully demonstrated this reorienting toward truth and forgiveness in response to the pain he has endured due to white supremacy. He wrote, "I will make sure this pain becomes forgiveness. And then I'll make sure that forgiveness becomes the wisdom to make sure no one uses the sermons of forgiveness to justify white supremacy [and] racism. . . . As a follower of Jesus I admit my pride and my unwillingness to listen to those who think differently." Forgiveness doesn't deny pain or accept abuse; rather, it equips us to turn away from judgments and toward truth.

Over the years, Jesus has been revealing my judgments and stereotypes of people as well as the false narratives that I've believed about myself. I've needed to repent and hear Jesus' truth:

> You don't just exist to help others, nor are you invincible. You need help too. No matter what you do, where you go, or who you disappoint: you are God's beloved child in whom God is well pleased. It's important to take care of yourself regardless of how useful you are to others. You are invited to live life abundantly.

[Forgiveness] releases us from the ties that bind us to our offender and it puts us in a position to freely receive God's forgiveness and fellowship.
JOHN PERKINS

As I hear this from Jesus, I'm freer to take care of myself and to love others from a healthier place. No longer am I driven to give out of a need to be needed, to have my worth validated, or to have my white guilt appeased. I get to give, to serve, to love out of the abundance of what I receive. I have permission to receive God's love for me, to rest, to play, to delight, and to be delighted in.

For me, listening to Jesus was a new experience and a bit intimidating. Slowly I've learned to recognize his voice in a myriad of settings. Sometimes I've felt his prompting toward truth during meetings with my spiritual director. At other times, the still, small voice has come into my consciousness as I wash the dishes. As I've welcomed Jesus to speak to me, I've experienced a profound shift in my beliefs. I've also had the gift of witnessing astounding changes in other people as they heard truth from Jesus that countered lies they'd believed. When they spoke a lie of worthlessness to Jesus and he replaced it with words they needed to know in a way they needed to hear, something shifted in a deep place beyond cognitive acceptance.

> *When you feel [Jesus'] merciful embrace . . . that's when life can change, because that's when we try to respond to the immense and unexpected gift of grace, a gift that is so overabundant it may even seem "unfair" in our eyes.*
> **POPE FRANCIS**

The ministry *Restoring the Foundations* shares a few inner-healing prayers: prayers of confession, forgiveness, renouncing the lie, and choosing to receive a new belief that Jesus reveals. (See "Replacing False Beliefs" in appendix two for an example prayer exercise.)

WALKING IT OUT

After embracing truth, we need to make practical changes so we can experience the new truths and rewire our brains. We need to know what it feels like to say no and to survive people's disappointment in order to try again. We need to taste refreshment and rest to begin prioritizing it in our lives.

As a step toward recovery, I needed to implement better boundaries by saying no or at least "not right now." (We'll explore this more in the next chapter.) Although I was required to carry a phone and be available 24/7, I could choose a different response to some of the requests that came at me throughout the day. I could empower staff to make decisions that they had the capability and authority to make. I could ask for help.

I also had to take a lunch break. It wasn't optional; it was necessary. When I did occasionally go for a walk or take thirty minutes in a coffee shop outside the residential facility, I returned to work more energized. I felt centered, connected to God, and more myself. Taking a lunch break didn't detract from my productivity; it actually enhanced it. I also wasn't as grouchy when I got home in the evening, and I was better able to let go of the weight of the work and release it into the hands of Jesus. Allowing myself a break grounded me in my belovedness, and it gave me perspective and space to breathe. I was able to notice what I was feeling and experiencing. I was freer to make the changes I needed to make, because I knew that my identity and acceptance weren't based on what I did and how people received me.

For myself, implementing lunch breaks, walks, and deep breathing exercises has been a critical component of my recovery journey. For others, different practices may be more effective. One of my close friends returned to the United States after living internationally in a community that dealt with systemic violence and insecurity. She was diagnosed with PTSD and carried secondary trauma from work abroad and prior work with women caught in cycles of abuse in the United States. For her, therapy along with adopting consistent practices of yoga, prayer, and gardening were the first steps toward slowing down, paying attention to her anxiety, and beginning to explore the path toward healing. She shared, "Making time and space for gardening connected me with the metaphor of life and growth coming out of darkness in a way that nothing else had connected. I experienced God's love for me through watching the plants grow from the soil, gain life, and produce fruit. It began to free me from old chains of guilt and fear. It gave space to heal some of the anger I felt."

For each individual, the practices may look different. Through prayer and the support of a therapist or trusted friend, listen to yourself. Pay attention to what those "slowing down" practices might look like for you. Is it adopting a new kind of prayer practice? Is it finding a dance studio? In the next section, we will explore more ways to thrive by living into our changing beliefs and behavior.

REFLECTION QUESTIONS

- Review the stages of change. How are you doing with your desire to take better care of yourself?
- Name one of your double binds that blocks you from taking care of yourself. Work through the above Double Bind exercise—the complete handout is found at genesisprocess.org/process-descriptions.
- Consider the role of therapy in your life. What are the barriers? In addition to more traditional talk therapy, is there another form of therapy that is attractive and accessible? A few examples are Art, Music, Dance, Equine, Horticulture, and Somatic Therapy.

EXERCISES

- Invite a trusted friend, spiritual director, or pastor to pray with you through the "Replacing False Beliefs" prayer exercise in appendix two.
- Reflect on "Patient Trust," a poem by Pierre Teilhard de Chardin.
- Practice a breath prayer or Five Senses Walk; see appendix one.

RECOMMENDED RESOURCES

Anatomy of the Soul by Curt Thompson

The Wounded Heart: Hope for Adult Victims of Childhood Sexual Abuse by Dan Allender

The Body Keeps the Score: Brain, Mind, and the Body In the Healing of Trauma by Bessel van der Kolk

My Grandmother's Hands: Racialized Trauma and the Pathway to Mending Our Hearts and Bodies by Resmaa Menakem

PART FOUR

THRIVING

The glory of God is a human being fully alive.

ST. IRENAEUS

TWELVE

DISCERNING WHEN TO SAY NO AND WHEN TO SAY YES

Workers who continue to take on duties that aren't theirs will eventually burn out. It takes wisdom to know what we should be doing and what we shouldn't. We can't do everything.

DR. HENRY CLOUD AND JOHN TOWNSEND, *BOUNDARIES*

When I first started working at Tierra Nueva, I moved into a house with four other women. One woman had been living in her van for more than ten years. Bridget was in her upper sixties, affected by mental health issues, and in need of a warmer place to pass the winter. Longing to follow Jesus' radical hospitality to those on the margins, my roommates and I invited her to live with us.

In the minds of many, welcoming her into our house was crazy. In all honesty, it didn't go so smoothly and only lasted a few months. She dropped cans of white paint down the stairwell, pawned my friend's bike, and terrified us all with her near misses at burning down the house: the time she heated it by leaving the oven door open, or the time she spliced space heater wires to an extension cord, and placed the heater in our carport on top of ice covered with blankets.

My relationship with her was one of the most challenging relationships of my life. It was also a huge gift. Alongside many other staff and friends, I loved her—and she occasionally infuriated me—over the following ten years before she passed away. I longed for her to pursue life and wholeness, but I found out quickly that I couldn't change her.

In many ways Bridget taught me that I can't do it all, that I can't fix or save people. She helped expose my codependency and revealed to me that God moves outside of me. I learned the importance of not doing everything for someone, discerning when to say yes and when to say no, and helping others take actions that *they* choose and are capable of. We used to say that she was the informal trainer of our new advocates, because she taught us about life on the street, about homelessness, and about boundaries.

When we're living out of belovedness, we're able to respond out of freedom and connection to God and ourselves. To thrive, we need to examine how our underlying beliefs and secondary trauma affects our ability to discern thoughtful responses.

EMBRACE LIMITS

A prominent false belief driving an inability to say no is "We can handle anything." When we believe we're limitless in our energy and compassion, we also believe that boundaries are signs of weakness. Greg McKeown leads trainings for businesses and nonprofits on what he calls *essentialism:* being guided by our values and subsequent priorities. He calls people who think they don't need boundaries *nonessentialists*, adding,

> Without limits, they eventually become spread so thin that getting anything done becomes virtually impossible. Essentialists, on the other hand, see boundaries as empowering. They recognize that boundaries protect their time from being hijacked. . . . They know that clear boundaries allow them to proactively eliminate the demands and encumbrances from others that distract them from the true essentials.

As humans, we have limits. It is not weak to acknowledge our limits and needs. This allows us to make room for important interactions. We might receive help from others, empower others to do something they might not believe they're able to do, and work more effectively and compassionately. Brené Brown offers the question, "What boundaries do I need to put in place so I can work from a place of integrity and extend the most generous interpretations of the intentions, work, and actions of others?" We need to remember that we can only do so much. We aren't responsible for how other people respond or what choices they make. When we know our limits, we can better estimate how to use our time and be more available when we're with people.

Bridget was persuasive and good at asking for what she wanted. After years of knowing her and saying yes to her many requests, I became more discerning—and more grounded in my identity through post-burnout recovery. One afternoon, she called while I was at home, asking for a favor. I had switched to working part-time to care for my baby, and although I had regular office hours, I sometimes responded outside of those set hours. She wanted me to pick her up an hour away, drive to her bank an hour south, and then take her to three other places. She explained that I was the only one who could help with this "emergency." All this would require about four hours of driving. In the past I would have been quickly pulled into her crisis. Her need would call out my desire to be useful.

Instead I took a moment to think and decided it was too much and not necessary for me to jump at this request. I told her I couldn't, it was too far to drive, and I needed to be home with my daughter. She replied, "Bring her with you!" I briefly considered the idea of driving for hours with my baby, stopping to nurse her in some bank parking lot. And I almost allowed her to convince me it was possible. Her desperation was clear, and her conviction that I was the only one who could help pulled at my heartstrings, my sense of purpose, and my desire to be helpful. I'm a two on the Enneagram, after all. It's like she knew how to get to me.

Fortunately I shook myself out of it. I realized there were other options she could pursue, and her need wasn't actually urgent. So I turned her down again. She later called me and exuberantly recounted how she had succeeded at her errands. In this situation, not only was I able to be at home and present with my baby, but she was also empowered to find other creative and resourceful ways to care for her own needs. It was a constant practice to discern when and what was actually helpful and supportive.

Again, when we base our worth on how well we succeed at helping people, setting limits feels like failure. The more we fear disappointing people, the more boundaryless we become. This dilemma presents another double bind. So let's practice by exploring the exercise from chapter eleven.

If I say no appropriately, people might be mad at me, they might not like me, and they might even reject me. I'll feel unhelpful and incapable. It'll affect my identity as a helper, so I'll feel like a failure. On the other hand, I'll have more time. I won't feel bound to something because of guilt and false responsibility. I'll feel freer and less anxious, and I'll be able to say yes and mean it.

If I'm not able to respond with either a yes or a no in any given situation, I'll relapse into old codependent behavior. I'll get exhausted and stressed out, and I'll experience repercussions on my health. I might burn out. The person I'm trying to help might become overly dependent on me and won't feel empowered. I might enable unhealthy behavior. On the other hand, people might be pleased at how "helpful" I am.

Reflect on your reasons for not wanting to say no or yes.

- What do I believe about myself? About my role?
- How much does a desire to please others affect my ability to say yes or no to requests?
- What fears are driving my behavior?
- What might it be like to give myself permission to say no, to avoid being drawn into a crisis, or to choose not to help out of guilt?

EMBRACE COMPLEXITY

Although some struggle to say no, others protect themselves by creating rigid rules and boundaries that guide their responses. They say no to requests and ask for time off without feeling guilty and worried about how it affects others. They set personal rules such as "I never take on a coworker's responsibilities—even if the need arises."

When we're exhausted and burning out, it's common to swing to extremes—always saying yes or always saying no. Laura van Dernoot Lipsky names this as a common trauma exposure response: the inability to embrace complexity. We're either captive to the needs of others or bound to organizational regulations. We lack the energy and capacity to discern critically and to respond thoughtfully. Trauma affects the brain's capacity to stay in the gray and perhaps find an alternative solution, a third way.

Clear-cut rules make sense in a lot of professions and are necessary during seasons of ministry as well. They're also beneficial when we are in recovery from codependent workaholism and don't have the energy or clarity to make decisions. Post-burnout, I needed to protect my sabbath because I didn't have the energy to debate whether or how to respond.

> *Oftentimes the boundaries of our lives allow us to experience life more fully.*
> **DR. BRIAN BANTUM**

Following fixed rules is straightforward. It's more challenging to discern and listen. Even protecting sabbath can't be the utmost principle. Jesus himself repeatedly broke the Sabbath rules of the day to heal and care for those around him. He responded to crises in ways that didn't please people but led them to know and to experience God. At times he chose not to respond as quickly as people wanted him to: He rested in the storm. He said no to requests. He went up to the mountain to pray, even when there were crowds of people in need surrounding him.

For those of us who have a hard time saying no, it's helpful to remember that every time we say yes to something, we say no to something else. Often what we're saying no to isn't at first apparent. Sometimes we say no to peace, to time by ourselves, to being with people in our inner circle, to having margins in our lives. In the next chapter, we'll look at integrating transition practices as part of our rhythms of rest. Creating margins before responding to requests enables us to say no and yes appropriately. To be aware of what's going on in us and to set healthy boundaries, we need to slow down and invite God's guidance.

Sometimes situations call for maintaining the rules. Others warrant flexibility. We often need wisdom and discernment to figure out how to respond. When I'm in a healthy place, it's easier to listen to what I need, to hear what another is asking for, and to be led by God in the messiness.

INVITE GOD TO GUIDE

When working at Tierra Nueva's Family Support Center, I received many requests from people to address urgent hardships. We had a few clear-cut guidelines on how to use our limited emergency funds. However, many of our decisions were situational. People often came in asking for an emergency motel stay. For the majority of those who asked, we chose not to pay for motels and instead worked with them toward longer-term housing and recovery. It would've been easier to have a simple rule about this, but we sought to be led by God.

One afternoon, my coworker called me about a couple that was asking for a motel stay. I was just about to drive an hour south to Seattle to be with my family. I was tired, ready for a break, and wrapping up work for the week. It would have been easy to just say no. However, we had been talking about praying together before making decisions, so we took a moment on the phone to listen to God. Surprisingly, we both felt prompted to meet this couple and pay for a motel night, contrary to our normal procedure.

A bit reluctant and hoping it wasn't going to take too long, I drove to the rundown motel where the couple was waiting. I thought I would just say hello, find out a bit about them, tell them about Tierra Nueva, and pay the motel. Instead the couple was being kicked out and needed to move to a different motel. Together we loaded up their ten bags, skateboard, and little dog into my '85 Volvo, and we drove down the highway to the other cheap motel in town. On the way, I got to hear more of their story. The woman had attended one of our jail Bible studies the previous year. When they were scanning "Churches" in the phone book, she recognized Tierra Nueva and decided to call. They both said they wanted to change and expressed interest in learning more about our ministry. I offered to pray with the couple, and they eagerly accepted. I invited them to church that week, but doubted I would see them again.

Little did I know that this was the beginning of God connecting them to our ministry for years to come. They are the Rileys, whose recovery journey I shared about in chapter eight. They are now pastors and jail chaplains who have three healthy kids and stable housing, and they have become dear friends. Despite my reluctance, by God's grace I got to participate with God in their story. If I had acted on impulse or let my exhaustion guide my decision, I would have quickly turned down their motel request. I also would have missed out on the delight of knowing them and witnessing their transformation.

God's leading isn't always clear. Often we cry out and don't hear. We question. We respond to subtle nudges. Sometimes we walk forward until there is a red light. Acknowledging my own finitude and dependency on God enables me to maintain a posture of openness and receptivity to God's leading. This process also includes learning to trust my gut as I grow in confidence that what I'm hearing is worth moving forward on. It has been freeing to seek to be led by God and to respond to what God invites me to do—not just what I think needs to be done or feel pressured to do. I'm also overwhelmed by gratitude that God works through me and yet is not dependent on me.

> *Prayer requires that we stand in God's presence with open hands, naked and vulnerable, proclaiming to ourselves and to others that without God we can do nothing.*
>
> HENRI NOUWEN

RECOGNIZE GOD'S MOVEMENT OUTSIDE OF YOU

Those in Christian social justice circles often talk about building God's kingdom and being God's hands and feet in the world. These ideas kickstart many people into doing something for others. They also made sense to me and called me into action. However, they eventually became a burden and contributed to my messiah complex.

If we view ourselves as the builders, we risk idolizing our efforts and impact, enlisting God as *our* assistant helping *us* to build God's kingdom. This belief connotes that it's up to us. Unconsciously I began to think that if I didn't respond to a particular need, no one would. I also assumed that figuring out how and when to help people was up to me. The solutions I came up with on my own were limited and were often affected by my needs and desires. I didn't know how to lean into God for guidance in decisions.

In contrast, God is described as the builder throughout Scripture. Our work is in vain if we think we're the builders. As Danielle Shroyer wrote, "Repairing the world doesn't demand us to be saviors; only participants." God invites us to be colaborers in kingdom work. We're called to *seek* God's kingdom, not *build* it. God is the ultimate actor, initiator, and laborer.

Although our actions do make a difference, both positive and negative, God isn't limited and isn't dependent on us. When asked about their recovery journey, the Rileys credit it all to God. They recognize God as the ultimate actor and healer. Yes, we gave them rides, visited them in jail, and provided relapse prevention counseling. In some ways, we were God's hands and feet. God worked through us, despite our ineptitude. Yet God loved and ministered to them far beyond our capacity. What would've happened if I had said no to their motel request that afternoon and continued on my way? I trust that God would have met them somehow. And maybe I'm the one who would've missed out.

As we discern our responses, we get to trust that God is at work with those we accompany and has even more in store for people than we can ask or imagine. God sees each person as beloved—not how our jaded, tired, and disbelieving eyes might see them. This doesn't mean we don't act, push ourselves, or love when it's uncomfortable. We're invited to listen, to be led by God, and not to make decisions out of fear, anxiety, or trauma exposure. God is alive and moving despite and beyond our efforts.

REFLECTION QUESTIONS

- How do your potential risk factors for codependency and workaholism affect your boundaries and ability to say yes and no?
- What false beliefs are driving your discernment and freedom to say yes and no?

EXERCISES

- Revisit one of the listening prayer exercises found in appendix two: Garden Wall, Surrendering Burdens, or Moving Beyond Codependency.
- Take a glance at the "Guideline for Living" in appendix two in preparation for the next chapter.

RECOMMENDED RESOURCES

Essentialism: The Disciplined Pursuit of Less by Greg McKeown
Boundaries by Henry Cloud and John Townsend
The New Codependency by Melody Beattie
Always Enough by Heidi and Rolland Baker

THIRTEEN

CREATING RHYTHMS OF REST AND RENEWAL

Abide in me as I abide in you. Just as the branch cannot bear fruit by itself unless it abides in the vine, neither can you unless you abide in me. I am the vine, you are the branches. Those who abide in me and I in them bear much fruit, because apart from me you can do nothing.

JOHN 15:4-5

A few years ago, my husband and I walked a segment of the Camino de Santiago, an ancient pilgrimage route to Santiago de Compostela in northwestern Spain. Our path wound through small towns surrounded by field after field of grapevines. As I walked, I sensed God inviting me to notice the vines and branches. The thick, gnarly vines rose up sturdily out of the earth. From their tops, tender green branches spread, networking across trellises, bursting forth with large clumps of grapes. The contrast was stark: new fragile life sprouting from old, solid vines. It was clear that branches needed to stay connected to the vine. Without that vine, the branches would quickly wither and die, and there would be no fruit.

I don't think Jesus was criticizing us when he said that we can't do anything without him (John 15:5); he was simply stating the reality. We need to be connected to our Source just as the branches need to be connected to the vine. We need God's wisdom, nourishment, and life flowing through us.

In the gospel story of Mary and Martha, Jesus challenged Martha's complaint about her sister Mary, sitting as his feet while she was bustling about in the kitchen. Jesus said, "Martha, Martha, you are worried and distracted by many things; there is need of only one thing. Mary has chosen the better part, which will not be taken away from her" (Luke 10:41-42).

I confess I want Jesus' core message in this passage to be this: serve me but without anxiety. However, he took it a step further. Being with Jesus is the better choice—and the only thing that is necessary.

Jesus invites us to spend time with him, to lean on him, and to be nourished by him—not just to serve him. We're loved not for what we do but for who we are. Father Greg Boyle describes abiding in Jesus as an invitation to "marinate in the intimacy of God." He writes, "Jesus chose to marinate in the God who is always greater than our tiny conception, the God 'who loves without measure and without regret.' To anchor yourself in this, to keep always before your eyes this God is to choose to be intoxicated, marinated in the fullness of God." To live out of our belovedness, we need to soak in the abundant love that God offers us.

Developing rhythms of rest is not a new concept. As I became aware of how codependent I was, how much I lived out of my false beliefs, and how impacted I was by secondary trauma, ancient practices took on a new life and importance. God demonstrated and enacted a day of rest from the very beginning, inviting—even commanding—his people to do likewise. However, instead of God's command causing me to feel guilty, I've become thirsty to know and develop sustainable rhythms of rest. I still forget and go back to old habits, but I'm aware of the importance of rhythms, and I notice more quickly what is lacking.

Regular rhythms are highlighted across a wide audience. Lin Manuel-Miranda started writing morning and evening encouragements to his Twitter followers. Here's one: "Before you let the world in, make a little space for yourself. Cup of coffee, tidy the counter, morning quiet." His thoughts meant so much to people that he complied them in a book, *Gmorning, Gnight! Little Pep Talks for Me & You.*

Spirituality is included as one of the core components of resilience in a variety of sources. Psychologist Dr. Zelana Montminy emphasizes spirituality in her book *21 Days to Resilience*, writing, "Spirituality influences how we react to stressful situations and how well we recover from trauma." She cites various studies published in the periodicals *Psychology of Religion and Spirituality, Aging and Mental Health* and *ISRN Psychiatry* that show that spirituality is connected to improved physical and mental health.

While I was recovering from burnout and developing my spiritual practices, books that I wouldn't have touched before have become essential to my journey. I've read rich resources on spiritual disciplines and rhythms of rest, some of which are mentioned at the end of this chapter. I won't try to offer a new treatise on spiritual disciplines. Rather I'll address some of the core ideas that have helped reorient my understanding of rest and its importance for wounded healers.

First, consider your own associations and practices:

- What negative or positive associations do you have with spiritual practices or rhythms?
- What current or past spiritual practices have been life-giving to you?
- What benefits do you receive from these rhythms?
- What are your challenges in relation to engaging in these rhythms?

BENEFITS OF A DAILY PRACTICE

Throughout this book we've explored how our identity affects resilience in our work. Creating space for a daily practice connects us to our source of value and love. It reminds us that we are more than what we accomplish. Henri Nouwen wrote, "We discover that being is more important than having, and that we are worth more than the results of our efforts. . . . When you are able to create a lonely place in the middle of your actions and concerns, your successes and failures slowly can lose some of their power over you." As I hear the voice of the Beloved, the voice of Love, I drop my defenses. I am free to be weak, to be accepted as I am, to receive help. I am reminded that I'm not alone, that I belong, that it isn't all up to me, and that I am loved regardless.

In the midst of so much to do, it seems counterintuitive to set aside time for a daily practice. However, as I shared in the previous chapter, taking a lunch break actually made me more alive and productive. Father Thomas Keating, founder of Contemplative

Outreach, encourages a prayerful daily practice not despite but because of our busyness. The busier we are, the more we need to have times of prayer, because it's hard to get off "the treadmill" of "excessive activity."

When we have a daily practice, Father Keating explains, we're often able to do what we have to do with greater effectiveness and joy. Without it, "we run on cylinders that are out of oil or a bit rusty. Our powers of giving are pretty well used up by noon on most days. Contemplative prayer opens [us] to the power of the Spirit. [Our] capacity to keep giving all day long increases. [We're] able to adjust to difficult circumstances and even to live with impossible situations."

We need to be filled, nourished, and grounded in truth each day to counter the many voices, pressures, and pulls that demand our attention. Without that, we fall back into the spiral of shame, we relapse into codependent rescuing behavior, and we think it's all up to us. Stopping is an act of rebellion to the voices that tell us we are loved for what we do.

According to Shanesha Brooks-Tatum, for people of color—especially Black women—stopping and caring for self is a subversive act. She writes,

> For centuries Black women worldwide have been taking care of others, from the children of slave masters to those of business executives, and often serving today as primary caregivers for the elderly as home health workers and nursing home employees. Black women's self-care is also subversive because to take care of ourselves means that we disrupt societal and political paradigms that say that Black women are disposable, unvalued.

While living in Haiti, a priest named Father Tom recounted his own daily practice to journalist Gerard Thomas Straub, who said,

"He candidly told me that he could not survive without his early morning prayer time."

Father Tom explained:

> There are times in my work among the chronically poor of the world that I'm left with a feeling of hopelessness. . . . I sense within people a fatigue of compassion. The need is so great that our humble efforts to help seem woefully inadequate. The only way for me to chase away the hopelessness is to spend time in prayer every day. Prayer is a lifeline to hope.

> *Caring for myself is not self-indulgence, it is self-preservation, and that is an act of political warfare.*
> AUDRE LORDE

A daily practice benefits us not only spiritually but also emotionally, psychologically, and physically. In a recent *New York Times* article, psychologist Dr. David DeSteno wrote, "An emerging body of research shows that ritualistic actions, even when stripped from a religious context, produce effects on the mind ranging from increased self-control to greater feelings of affiliation and empathy."

As a result, choosing a daily practice is core to Lipsky's framework for cultivating *Trauma Stewardship*—and not accumulating trauma. She wrote, "A practice is not just a healthy option; it is our best hope of creating a truly sustainable life for ourselves." When taking her class "Self-Care for Social Workers," I was increasingly aware of how much I was being impacted by secondary trauma. In exasperation and feeling close to burnout, I asked her, "How do you keep from accumulating trauma?" She asked me what my daily practice was and invited me to double it. Whatever it is, the important thing is to do it daily, if not twice a day.

In recent years, I've been pressing into contemplative practices, such as lectio divina and Centering Prayer. When I first started practicing Centering Prayer, my mind raced and I ended up feeling frustrated and ashamed. I soon found that I needed to create some guidelines, such as not checking email before prayer time. I also needed to learn that creating the space for thoughts to surface and be released to God is part of contemplation.

Curt Thompson, MD, explained how focused attention exercises, such as Centering Prayer, can increase our ability to focus at other times in the day as well. We're invited to notice our distracted and anxious thoughts, offer them to God, and extend ourselves grace.

Scripture often invites us to practice being still in God's presence. Spiritual directors Christine Valters Paintner and Lucy Wynkoop write, "Stillness can renew and refresh us because for a few moments we are able to release our compulsive *doing*. Our culture tells us we are valuable when we perform, produce, or achieve. God tells us we are valuable as we are."

Learning to *be* and not *do* is the heart of the struggle for many of us. God doesn't need us to do anything. Contemplative prayer is a way I am learning to come without agenda, except to sit in God's presence, to practice being loved regardless of what I do. Although my mind wanders, I'm invited to return with grace to a word that grounds me in truth. These practices free me from striving so I can recenter, surrender to God, and be reminded that it isn't all up to me. When abiding in God, I'm more grounded and can actually be more effective while also being sustained with joy.

INTEGRATING A DAILY PRACTICE

Daily practices have ebbed and flowed in different seasons of my life. While writing this book, I became a mama, so my life and rhythms have certainly changed. Practicing what I preach has taken on a whole new dimension. No longer can I choose when I want to have a time of silence and prayer, though it's still essential for me.

I attempted various practices during my oldest daughter's first couple of years. While she was an infant, I wrote a nursing prayer to help me connect to God while caring for her. As she grew older, and we had a second child, I've continued to try and set aside fifteen to twenty minutes a day for prayer. Although there are dishes to wash, laundry to do, emails to respond to, and this book to write, stopping and spending time with God reorients me to who I am as a beloved daughter. Sometimes it's while rocking the youngest to sleep. Even so, it helps me to know I am loved regardless of how I contribute to this world or how I parent my daughters. It's essential for me to practice slowing down, because I tend to maintain a quick pace, have a hard time settling down, and easily lose touch with my needs. Here is a simple framework that has been helpful:

- Do something that works for you, for this season.
- Start small.
- Maintain two key elements: life-giving and daily.
- When ready, add in a weekly, quarterly, and yearly rhythm.

Some daily practice ideas include prayer, breathing, listening to a song, coloring, exercise, journaling, reading, and walking. Although solitude isn't possible in all stages of life, I encourage pressing into connection with God at some point every day, even if others are in the room or are being pushed in a stroller.

Integrating practices and margins during the day frees us from burdens we aren't intended to carry. When we mindlessly move from one appointment to the next or from work to home, we bring whatever we're carrying with us. Greg McKeown calls margins a buffer. He gives the example of a buffer zone at the periphery of a protected environmental land that creates "extra space between that area and any potential threats that might infiltrate it." We too need buffer zones so we can care for ourselves and diminish potential threats to our well-being.

Providing space for margins frees us to reflect on our identity as beloved. In Lorie Martin's book of prayer exercises, *Invited*, there is an exercise called "Transition Times." It encourages readers to "become aware of God being with you" during the transitions between daily activities. We all have numerous daily transitions: upon waking up, when going to work, between appointments, during lunch breaks, on the way home, and before going to bed. During these times, we can add short, intentional practices, such as washing our hands, walking around the block, taking three deep breaths, or free-writing for even five minutes after an appointment.

Transition activities don't have to be huge time consumers but rather can be simple activities that engage the senses and reconnect you to yourself and to God.

A few years ago, a colleague gave me a little felted bowl with five stones in it. The idea was to hold the stones while identifying the burdens they represent, then mindfully laying each one down. I began calling it my Trust Bowl. It's not necessary to use stones; you could write names of people you're working with or feel burdened by on small pieces of paper. At the end of the day, pick each one up, and then lay each back down in the bowl one at a time. As you do so, bless the person and surrender them to Jesus.

The Ignatian prayer practice of examen at the end of the day is another way to reflect and offer to God our gratitude, needs, and confessions. In examen, we express gratitude as well as lament for evading God's presence during the day. It is also a way we can practice emotional awareness. Kevin O'Brien, SJ, incorporates "Praying over the Significant Feelings of the Day" into examen. He wrote,

> Ignatius believed that God communicates with us not only through our mental insight but also through our "interior movements" as he called them: our feelings, emotions, desires, attractions, repulsions, and moods. As you reflect on the day, you may notice some strong feelings arise. . . . Did they draw you closer to God? . . . Or did the feelings lead you away from God, make you less faithful, hopeful, and loving?

After a workshop I led on trauma-informed soul care, Rosemary Crawford, a therapist who works with perpetrators and victims of domestic violence, developed a new practice for transitions between appointments and before going home. She gave me permission to share it with you.

> As we were talking about the impact of vicarious trauma, Bethany mentioned the word *saturated*, and I immediately wrote it down. I'm hired to be a sponge—porous to the experiences of others—so I know what it feels like to be saturated. But instead of trying to be a bigger sponge all the time (taking in more and more content, complexity, feelings, trauma, and stories with no relief), I need to have a ritualized reminder to wring out my soul on a daily basis.
>
> With this in mind, I decided to buy a sponge to help me with the beautiful burden of helping others sort through themselves. Between each appointment, I splashed my sponge with a few drops of water. At the end of the day, I wrung it out in my watering can and blessed my office plants with the remnants of my liquidated energy. This personal rain ritual turns tears into acknowledgment of the hard work my clients and I are doing. In addition, my plants return the love to all who enjoy the space.

> Since starting this ritual, I've found more relief, more ease in the transition between my office and my home. After a long day, I find it easier to laugh, to listen to my loved ones, and to have space for creativity.

Rosemary's simple yet profound practice beautifully demonstrates how a transition activity can bring much refreshment without taking much effort. Whatever the practice and whatever the time of day, may you allow space for yourself to be nourished.

REFRAMING A WEEKLY PRACTICE

Cease striving.
You are loved.
This is a day of love, of grace toward yourself, of delight.
It is a grounding day.
Let yourself move slowly, breathe deeply, notice, and relax.
Relax your body, your mind, tension, and let go of the to-do list.
You don't need to produce anything today.
You are—that is enough.
Notice your reactions with grace and humility.
Practice kindness; loving yourself and others.
This is Sabbath.
Don't hurry or worry.
Sabbath is a gift, a gift to be free, to live wholly,
a privilege indeed that not many experience.
Practice resurrection this day.
You don't need to do anything.

All too often I've found it challenging to settle down at the end of the week and lay aside the to-do list. It becomes a double bind, as I mentioned in chapter eleven. Frequently, as I sit with Jesus in those moments I sensed his gentle voice calling me to rest. In the same way that I've been learning to integrate a daily practice, I've also gained new appreciation for the importance of a weekly practice, or a day of rest.

Sabbath is an invitation, even a command, that continues from the Jewish tradition and the Old Testament into the New Testament. In the letter to the Hebrews, the author wrote, "So then, there remains a sabbath rest for the people of God, for whoever has entered God's rest has also rested from his works as God did from his. Let us therefore strive to enter that rest, so that no one may fall by the same sort of disobedience" (Hebrews 4:9-11 ESV). We're encouraged to strive to enter God's rest. And it isn't often that Scripture invites us to strive.

Sabbath doesn't require leaving our communities or the people we work with. For some that isn't possible. Similar to a daily practice, sabbath is a reorientation toward God and toward our true selves as beloved and human.

During the week, we often fall back into old habits, returning to live out of our false beliefs. We forget that we're loved simply for who we are. We may feel that everything *does* depend on us. In her book *Sacred Rhythms*, Ruth Haley Barton wrote,

> This is a grandiosity that we indulge to our own peril. . . . There is a freedom that comes from being who we are in God and resting in God that eventually enables us to bring something truer to the world than all of our doing. Sabbath keeping helps us to live within our limits, because on the Sabbath, in many different ways, we allow ourselves to be the creature in the presence of our Creator.

Read that last line again: "We allow ourselves to be the creature in the presence of our Creator."

Practicing sabbath is an act of trust in God that affirms our dependence on God. It moves us away from a messiah complex, connecting us to our true source and giving us a chance to reaffirm our identity as beloved children of God. It provides the opportunity to unpack the stories, lay down the burdens, and walk forward in freedom. It reminds us that we're loved no matter what.

To recover a sabbath practice, I took a deeper look at its essence: freedom to delight in God and in God's goodness. I then needed to implement guidelines for both a weekly and a daily practice.

SABBATH AS A DAY OF AND FOR DELIGHT

I used to love the first section of Isaiah 58 because I had a deep conviction and passion to set people free from the chains that bind them and to care for those in need. The beginning of that chapter beautifully articulates our call to sacrificially love our neighbor. However, not until a few years ago was I struck by the verses about the sabbath. Somehow I had overlooked them while viewing them through my zealous activist lens.

> If you refrain from trampling the sabbath,
>   from pursuing your own interests on my holy day;
> if you call the sabbath a delight
>   and the holy day of the LORD honorable;
> if you honor it, not going your own ways,
>   serving your own interests, or pursuing your own affairs;
> then you shall take delight in the LORD,
>   and I will make you ride upon the heights of the earth;
> I will feed you with the heritage of your ancestor Jacob,
>   for the mouth of the LORD has spoken. (Isaiah 58:13-14)

A sabbath isn't just intended to be a rule we follow for the sake of it or a day for self-interest or self-indulgence. It leads us to delight in the Lord, to be held and nourished by God's presence, and to love others. If we honor it, we soar.

Professor and therapist Dan Allender notes that delight can be our barometer for how we live into sabbath each week. He wrote, "Will this be merely a break or a joy? Will this lead my heart to wonder or routine? Will I be more grateful or just happy that I got something done?" How often have we viewed sabbath as either a break from work or a day to run errands? Treating sabbath as a time for delight can be revolutionary. It has freed me from striving to get things done and given me permission to let myself engage in what brings me delight.

With delight as our barometer, the sabbath is a day when we allow ourselves to do what's nourishing. It's a day when we refuse to get caught up in despair, busyness, or anxiety. Allender wrote, "We enter delight only as we gaze equally and simultaneously at creation and redemption, in spite of the darkness that surrounds us and constantly clamors to be truer than God." When we find ourselves going down the shame or worry spiral, may we hear the voice of the Beloved calling us to receive grace and love.

What an amazing thing it would be to have the rhythm of your life regularly usher you into such deep trust that you could actually rest from it all. Who would we be, who would I be, if I trusted like this for twenty-four hours once a week.

RUTH HALEY BARTON

Anthony de Mello is known for saying, "Behold the one beholding you and smiling." Marinating in this phrase, I turn my face from the cares and stresses of the world. I sense the Beloved smiling at me—the Beloved who carries and loves the world. God invites us to rest, to not just cease from working, but to be present to God being present and delighting in us.

As we practice sabbath, we're also invited to lean into sabbath rest for others. Sabbath isn't all about us. Our desire to love and care for others can be integrated into this day in a way that embodies God's delight in us and responds to God's invitation to love our neighbors. In practicing sabbath, we join with others around the globe and recognize our interconnectedness. It's a day of jubilee that reminds us of the ultimate jubilee. As Dan Allender said of the coming feast and play day, "Sabbath is day of delight for humankind, animals, and the earth; it is not merely a pious day and it is not fundamentally a break, a day off, or a twenty-four hour vacation. Sabbath is a feast day that remembers our leisure in Eden and anticipates our play in the new heavens and earth with family, friends, and strangers for the sake of the glory of God."

Theologian Walter Brueggemann explored this in his book *Sabbath as Resistance*.

> The way of *mammon* (capital, wealth) is the way of commodity that is the way of endless desire, endless productivity, and endless restlessness without any Sabbath. Jesus taught his disciples that they could not have it both ways. . . . [Jesus] becomes the embodiment of Sabbath rest for those who are no longer defined by and committed to the system of productiveness.

By resisting a culture driven by productivity, our choices have a ripple effect on those around us. We demonstrate that the way of Jesus involves restoration and jubilee for all people. By practicing sabbath, we demonstrate our dependency on God, this God who also chooses to rest.

Jesus told Martha that being with him is the one necessary thing. What does he mean by *necessary*? Necessary for our survival? For our well-being? For our life?

The rich language of Isaiah 58 has stuck with me as I've sought to understand more of the sabbath and how to take care of myself. I'm amazed by our God of love, who does not require that we *only* "seek justice." But as the prophet Micah said, we also "walk humbly with [our] God" (Micah 6:8).

CREATING A GUIDELINE FOR LIVING

As we covered in the previous chapter, acknowledging our limits and creating boundaries can help us to thrive. Many contemporary and early monastic communities have a rule of life, the best known being the Benedictine Rule. The word *rule* makes this practice sound restrictive and narrow. However, its intent is to center us throughout our daily life. The Northumbria Community states that the rule "serves as a framework for freedom—not as a set of rules that restrict or deny life, but as a way of living out our vocation alone and together. . . . It is a means to an end—and the end is that we might seek God with authenticity and live more effectively for Him."

Although rules or guidelines can be reminders to keep a sabbath, they aren't meant to usurp the core of the Sabbath. When Jesus healed the man with the withered hand on the Sabbath, he invited the man to stand in front of the synagogue. After looking intentionally around the room, making sure everyone was watching, he asked the man to stretch out his hand. And it was healed. Instead of erupting with applause, the crowd erupted with fury. Jesus had broken the rule. Yet Jesus wanted them to see this healing and to know that it's better to do good rather than harm on the Sabbath (Luke 6:9). Protecting the Sabbath isn't the goal, even though, as we saw in the previous chapter, strict rules are easier.

As we embark on integrating rhythms of rest, we must remember to do so with grace and love for ourselves. The primary orientation isn't toward what rules we want to implement but how we want to respond to God's invitation to delight in and be connected to ourselves, to God, and to community.

Creating a "framework for freedom" can be a way of naming the practices and choices we want to have that will set us up for success. By creating a guideline, we don't have to figure things out each week. We can decide what works for us for this season and then reevaluate.

If you choose to develop a guideline for living, or a rule of life, consider in what ways you need care: physically, spiritually, psychologically, socially, intellectually, and emotionally. Avoid the temptation to neatly categorize activities in each area. Soul care involves tending to our whole integrated selves. When I go for a run, it clearly benefits me psychologically and physically. Running is also a way I connect with God, benefiting me emotionally and spiritually. It also benefits me socially; I return home better able to be present to my family. Keep this in mind as you consider the following questions, as well as those included in the Guideline for Living exercise, found in appendix two.

In the next chapter, we'll look at the gifts of joy, gratitude, and play. These core practices will continue to help us be rooted in our identity as beloved children of God and equipped to thrive in our life and work.

REFLECTION QUESTIONS

- What would give [you] the greatest sense of the abiding goodness of the Father's arms?
- What brings you delight?
- What do you need to feel nurtured, strong, and healthy?
- What practices are important because of who you are and your current life stage?

- In what ways can your sabbath practice also lead to sabbath rest for others?

EXERCISES

- Create a Trust Bowl (see appendix one).
- Develop a Guideline for Living (see appendix two).
- Review the prayers you may have developed earlier: daily prayer and breath prayer.
- Using lectio divina, read Isaiah 58. Notice your reactions and what words or phrases stand out to you.
- Meditate on Anthony de Mello's quote, "Behold the one beholding you and smiling."
- Take a silent retreat day. Go up to a mountain or an expansive place with a view, and pray. Spend time marinating in the presence of God.

RECOMMENDED RESOURCES

Lectio Divina: Contemplative Awakening and Awareness by Christine Valters Paintner and Lucy Wynkoop. See also contemplative outreach.org/wp-content/uploads/2013/02/lectiodivinabrochure _2018_0.pdf.

Open Mind, Open Heart by Thomas Keating. See also contempla tiveoutreach.org/centering-prayer-method/.

Sabbath by Dan Allender

Sabbath as Resistance: Saying No to the Culture of Now by Walter Brueggemann

This Day: Collected & New Sabbath Poems by Wendell Berry

Sacred Rhythms: Arranging Our Lives for Spiritual Transformation by Ruth Haley Barton

FOURTEEN

LIVING IN JOY

Be joyful though you have considered all the facts.

WENDELL BERRY, *MANIFESTO: THE MAD FARMER LIBERATION FRONT*

Joy can burst forth in the most unexpected places. When I was working at the domestic violence shelter, I remember arriving to work one cold afternoon feeling very low on energy and depressed. I was grumbling about the dark clouds and also feeling unsupported by those around me. As I drove up to the shelter, I wondered what I was going to be able to offer the women.

As I sat around the dinner table for our weekly support group that evening, I was amazed, inspired, and humbled by the ability of the women to choose gratitude in the midst of horrific circumstances. All of the women were experiencing homelessness because of their abusive partners. All were at the shelter because they were fearful of being found. Most of them had made dramatic life changes, hauling their kids from shelter to shelter and switching schools, doctors, churches, and other community connections. Some even had to change their names. Yet it was that circle of women that gave me renewed perspective and hope, demonstrating once again that the line between giver and receiver is blurred.

One woman shared, "I focus on the positive and shove aside anything that brings me down or distracts me from moving forward." Another said, "I have so much to be grateful for. I press on and find humor in what I've experienced." I listened to the women, stunned at their hope and positivity, aware of my privilege—health, finances, relational support, education, home, job, and car—things all the women longed for. Despite the obstacles and trauma, they were persevering and seeking the good in their situations.

That night, I was the one who needed to be in that group. I needed to witness their hope, taste their gratitude, and be given permission to enjoy life.

DRINKING THE CUP OF SORROW *AND* JOY

For too long, I believed that sorrow was the right and perhaps only emotional response. I remember reading *The Prophet* by Kahlil Gibran, and grasping onto his line, "the deeper that sorrow carves into your being, the more joy you can contain." When I despaired, which was often, I clung to this quote for hope.

> *In the dark, we see the stars.*
> ANNE LAMOTT

Maybe joy is possible even in the midst of suffering. Despite the hurdles for farmworker families working two jobs and navigating life in a foreign and often hostile context, laughter reverberated through their tiny migrant cabins and out of their trailer walls. Maybe suffering and joy can coexist, yet I was bewildered by the joy I witnessed.

In the spring of 2012, I was on the way to a ministry conference when I received a phone call from a woman I knew well. She told me she had just run in her socks to Tierra Nueva, fleeing her abusive boyfriend. She was asking for help.

She had repeatedly fled and then returned to her boyfriend, as many women do who are caught in the cycle of domestic violence. My heart broke—for this woman and her boyfriend.

During the time of worship at the conference, I sang "Break Every Chain" at the top of my lungs. I was desperate to see the chains of violence and abuse broken. In the midst of this grief, I received prayer from a total stranger after the service. This is part of what he prayed:

> The Lord says you have been faithful to petition, to be before me on these things. I also want to carry the load; I do not want you to carry the weight. The Lord is lifting that off of you right now . . . saying you have permission to smile and have joy. For some things we feel that sorrow is the right response, and there is a time for that. But it is not irreverent or inappropriate for you to be ridiculously full of joy, right now in this season. It's a supernatural joy and peace. David said the joy of the Lord is my strength. Receive joy as your strength.

I was blown away. It pinpointed the challenge I had been feeling: unable to cope and heavily burdened by the realities around me. And I felt very known and heard by God in prayer for this couple and others.

Following Jesus involves suffering *and* joy. Although he invites us to carry his cross, he also invites us to live in joy and be fully alive. He proclaimed that this is the reason he came: "The thief comes only to steal and kill and destroy. I came that they may have life, and have it abundantly" (John 10:10). As Jesus wept in the garden, he asked his disciples, "Can you drink this cup?" Henri

Nouwen was greatly impacted by this question and believed the cup includes sorrow and joy. "For anyone who has the courage to enter our human sorrows deeply, there is a revelation of joy, hidden like a precious stone in the wall of a dark cave. . . . The cup of life is the cup of joy as much as it is the cup of sorrow. It is the cup in which sorrows and joys, sadness and gladness, mourning and dancing are never separated."

God's joy is not a Pollyanna happiness that pretends everything is okay. It's a joy that looks darkness in the face and proclaims the Light is more powerful. It doesn't deny our grief. As we explored in chapter nine, we need to allow ourselves to feel, and we need to create spaces for lament. Nouwen wrote, "We need to be able to let our tears flow freely, tears of sorrow as well as tears of joy, tears that are as rain on dry ground." There's room for lament in the cup of life, which holds both joy and sorrow.

For those who've experienced much loss and suffering, joy seems to be an impossible reality. For others it's easier to identify glimpses of hope, beauty amid the ashes. Archbishop Desmond Tutu is known for his laughter and joy as much as he is also known as one who has experienced and witnessed much violence and oppression. In 2016, he engaged in a weeklong conversation exploring the nature of joy with the Dalai Lama. The two men, who have survived much oppression, testified that it's possible to hold much joy while enduring and even because of much sorrow. Tutu wrote, "Suffering is inevitable, but how we respond to that suffering is our choice. . . . We are fragile creatures, and it is from this weakness, not despite it, that we discover the possibility of true joy." Our pain can turn us inward, or it can lead us to connection with others. "The more we turn toward others, the more joy we experience, and the more joy we experience, the more we can bring joy to others."

We're invited to choose and experience joy in the midst of our circumstances. This is our gift, our kingdom perspective, given to us as the Spirit pours living water into our places of thirst and sorrow. This is the liminal tension we live in as citizens of the kingdom, holding the "already but not yet." God gives us:

> the oil of joy
> instead of mourning,
> and a garment of praise
> instead of a spirit of despair. (Isaiah 61:3 NIV)

Although there is pain and suffering, we're invited to proclaim God's goodness and experience God's joy. The prophet Habakkuk proclaimed in the midst of famine, "Though . . . the fields yield no food . . . yet I will rejoice in the LORD" (Habakkuk 3:17-18). Apostle Paul cried out to know Christ and his suffering, yet followed this by encouraging the church of Philippi to "Rejoice in the Lord always" (Philippians 4:4). Suffering and rejoicing are held in tension.

The invitation to praise God and practice thankfulness is a refrain throughout Scripture.

> Enter his gates with thanksgiving,
> and his courts with praise.
> Give thanks to him, bless his name. (Psalm 100:4)

We're told that something powerful happens as we experience the joy of the Lord. It gives us strength (Nehemiah 8:10). It enhances our perspective and grounds us deeper in truth. It sustains, nourishes, guides, and fills us. Joy is a fruit of the Spirit's presence in our lives (Galatians 5:22). The Spirit enables us to walk boldly and fearlessly, knowing that we're accompanied and empowered by God's presence within us, even as we journey through the valleys of the shadow of death. As the psalmist wrote, "I fear no evil; for you are with me . . . my cup overflows" (Psalm 23:4-5). As we follow Jesus through the valleys, we experience his overflowing cup and can abound with thanksgiving (Colossians 2:7).

Gratitude, praise, and thanksgiving lead us to joy. Kevin O'Brien, author of *The Ignatian Adventure*, writes, "For St. Ignatius, gratitude is the most important step on the spiritual journey. An attitude of gratitude, practiced often enough, helps us find God in all things and can transform the way we look at our life and at other people."

Choosing gratitude is a challenging discipline, especially in the face of much trauma and suffering. *What is there to be grateful for?* I often asked women in jail this same question that I asked women at the DV shelter. In the darkness of jail, being separated from their children and partners, not having freedom or knowing what's going to happen, the women there also astounded me with their answers. Many have told me they're grateful to have a roof over their head, to have food, a shower, and a warm blanket. They're grateful to be alive, grateful for other women in the pod, grateful for God's love. Dan Allender writes, "Gratitude opens the heart not only to wonder but to freedom." For the women who are able to choose gratitude, time in jail seems easier. The stress, anxiety, grief, and fear of the unknown are held in tension with what brings them life and joy.

From psychologists and social workers to self-help authors, many have explored the concept of gratitude. Something happens psychologically when we choose gratitude. It opens us up to receive, to lift our eyes above our circumstances, and to gain a new perspective. It is a daring act that, according to Nouwen, "transforms our past into a fruitful gift for the future, and makes our life, all of it, into a life that gives life." Choosing gratitude in the midst of sorrow is a powerful act that leads us to joy and freedom, even if we are in captivity. This choice doesn't come naturally. It must come from within, not conjured or faked but a true gift from the Holy Spirit.

> *Gratitude is the space of that radical self-giving and that presence of beauty in our lives without which even the struggle for justice would be crippled.*
> GUSTAVO GUTIÉRREZ

Gratitude is also a gift we give others. Even in small ways, it's easy for me to respond to people serving me with apology instead of gratitude. When I wake up to my husband playing with our girls and making breakfast, I notice my temptation to apologize for not being there, for not helping. Instead, he doesn't need or want an apology. Gratitude is what I can offer. I need to give myself permission to receive and experience rest, joy, and gratitude.

All of us are invited to God's fullness of life.

RECOGNIZE THE NEED FOR DELIGHT, PLAY, AND LAUGHTER

Recently, as I begin my midday centering practice after getting my daughters down for their naps, I sit down and eat a piece of dark chocolate. Instead of hurriedly eating it as I carry dishes or put things away, I sit down and enjoy it. I let it usher me into a transition activity, allowing myself to truly taste it.

In the past couple of chapters, we've looked at a few practices to help ourselves slow down and reconnect with ourselves and God. Normal everyday activities, such as walking, breathing, or eating, can be transformed into spiritual practices. The Five Senses Walk is one of the activities in the appendix that invites walking, slowly, and noticing what we see, smell, hear, taste, and touch. The first time I was invited to do a Five Senses Walk, I remember immediately noticing how counter it was to the way I usually walked—in haste and with my mind consumed in worries. In *The Gift of Wonder*,

Christine Aroney-Sine shares about her "awe-and-wonder" walks around her neighborhood. She also describes numerous creative, tangible activities, such as painting rocks and doodling, to help us connect with God.

Giving ourselves the freedom to create, play, and laugh are restorative ways to engage our bodies and live in joy. Much has been written about the healing gift of art. First Aid Arts is an organization that equips staff working with highly traumatized people in simple arts-based activities, including music, movement, and writing. Their trainings use "arts-based psychosocial resources to promote resilience and reduce the symptoms of post-traumatic stress." One of the benefits of these activities is simply helping people to delight and laugh.

Play and humor are increasingly noted as effective tools for developing resilience. They help us to relax and think more clearly, and they can even change our limbic response. What's more, they improve our ability to interact and connect with others. In *21 Days to Resilience*, Zelana Montminy wrote, "Humor creates a domino effect and in that way increases our social connectivity and trust, further strengthening our resilience muscle."

Laughter, like joy, may feel out of place in the midst of suffering. In her book *Trauma and Grace,* Serene Jones explored how grace might be exhibited in the midst of trauma and oppression: "We collectively need the release and rejuvenation of laughter; we need ways to take in and celebrate the ongoing gifts of life and the goofy joy that attends us as we make our way through the messy world of human fellowship."

Many who've endured much hardship and oppression have also retained the ability to laugh. India, a country with much social and economic disparity, is also now known as the birthplace of Laughter Clubs or Laughter Yoga. Laughter Clubs are spreading around the world as people learn the healing and stress-reducing gift of laughter. Founder Dr. Madan Kataria in Mumbai, India, claims that the benefits include a good mood, more laughter, stress-reduction, an improved quality of life, and a positive attitude in challenging times. I first learned about Laughter Clubs when I saw a sign on a club venue in Kolkata portraying fifty of laughter's possible health benefits. It's doubtful that all of these are scientifically proven, but the joy of laughing with others, whether formally or informally, is something we all can affirm.

Another instigator of play and laughter is *applied improvisation*. The word *improv* usually brings to mind actors in a theater. However, improvisation workshops for organizations are being utilized as ways to build resilience and improve communication. My first experience of an improv workshop was while I was working at the domestic violence shelter. I was amazed at the benefit on our individual and collective communication, creativity, and outlook through playing some intentional games together, so I invited the presenter to lead a workshop for Tierra Nueva staff. Through that workshop, David Westerlund, my coworker at the time, became a firm believer in the gifts of improv and started an organization to provide workshops for nonprofits, businesses, schools, and people who are incarcerated.

According to David, applied improvisation is primarily about "remembering how to play again." He says improv games help to "silence the inner critic and learn to trust oneself, experience being present, and let go of control." He adds,

> When we feel safe enough to play and be present to each other, when we are vulnerable and find ourselves supported, we experience trust, connection, and belonging. Joy organically emerges! All of this helps us to become more resilient

> individuals and teams, building confidence and agency to face the unknown together.

Improv moves us from a fixed agenda for another person to receptivity for what that person has to offer.

After tasting some of the gifts of improv during my burnout recovery, I joined an Improv 101 class. I had quit my job at the domestic violence shelter and started therapy, yet I needed something more. I nervously signed up for the class, knowing that I didn't want to perform improv, yet I wanted to step more fully into the freedom and release of play. The class was at the exact same time when I had been leading a domestic violence support group for two years. Improv was a welcome change; it helped me to let go of personal agendas, to receive the gifts that others have to offer, and to let myself laugh.

REFLECTION QUESTIONS

- What barriers keep you from giving yourself permission to play and laugh?
- What are some practices that you have enjoyed at different points in your life simply for pleasure and joy? What would it take to create space for those now?
- What does it mean for you that the joy of the Lord is your strength? How have you experienced joy as strength before?

EXERCISES

- Try a new creative or playful activity this week. Read a novel or watch a movie for fun; bake or create something new; paint, giving yourself freedom to not create anything in particular; listen to a favorite song; play an instrument; sing or dance!

- Watch these videos on YouTube: "Laughter Yoga" or "Archbishop Desmond Tutu laughing."
- Try the Five Senses Walk or Breath Prayer in appendix one.

RECOMMENDED RESOURCES

The Gift of Wonder by Christine Aroney-Sine
One Thousand Gifts by Ann Voskamp
The Book of Joy: Lasting Happiness in a Changing World by the Dalai Lama and Desmond Tutu, with Douglas Abrams
First Aid Arts, www.firstaidarts.org/trainings-and-workshops

CONCLUSION

We are a container for God's loving presence in the world, always available, longing to be made known to us. . . . When God dwells in us fully, we carry God into each relationship and experience. We are not only restored, we are a blessing to others, bearing God's love in our daily surroundings.

JOYCE RUPP, *THE CUP OF OUR LIFE*

As I spent time recovering from burnout during my sabbatical, I wrestled with the question of my capacity. I was unsure how compassion fatigue would affect my future career choices. Did I have the emotional capacity to continue to do the work I loved, walking alongside people who had experienced immense emotional trauma? Had I accumulated too much secondary trauma, burned myself out, and ruined my capacity for good?

These questions churned in me while I took time away and sought to discern my next steps. They put me in a crisis of calling that was existential in some ways. *Could I not be who I felt called to be?* I knew I was an Enneagram type two helper. I loved hearing people's stories. I felt drawn to walk with people who had been hit from all sides by violence, abuse, and trauma. The work had shaped me, filled me with grief, and wounded me. *Did I not have capacity to do that work anymore?*

Over one weekend, my husband and I went backpacking in the mountains to rest, discern, and pray. I often experience rest in places of natural beauty. As I stand amazed at the wonder and beauty of God, I'm reminded of my smallness in the midst of greatness.

As I sat on a rock in the mountains, staring at the southwest side of Mount Baker, I opened a handout, *Holding the Cup*, which I'd received at a recent retreat led by Lorie Martin. This exercise leads the user through listening-prayer questions as you hold a cup. I didn't have a true cup, just my scratched-up Nalgene water bottle, but thought I'd give it a go. To be honest, I didn't expect much. I wanted to connect with God and hear what God had to say, but I wasn't expecting this to be it.

Prompted by the questions, I began looking at my Nalgene. I noticed the shape and style, the scratches and dents, and the peeling duct tape that I had hastily put on before an overseas trip, thinking it might come in handy. I laughed as I held it, remembering the places it had been.

I began asking God some of the questions on the handout, including this one: *What does God want to say about my uniqueness?* In the same way that the water bottle is unique, I am incredibly unique, with my own markings and woundings. I too have dents and scratches.

I followed the prayer exercise's invitation to continue holding the cup and to reflect on the following:

Fear not, I have called you by name,
you are Mine, you are precious
and honored in My sight . . .
I love you.

Those are good and often hard words to grasp fully: God has called me and accepts me as I am. It's a discipline for me to practice receiving God's acceptance. I'm still learning to do so with wonder and gratitude. As I sat among the surrounding mountains, which reminded me how small I am and yet so beloved by God, I began working through my resistance and welcoming God's love and acceptance.

The next section of the prayer exercise invited me to "recognize the cup as a container." As I looked at my Nalgene, I realized that the dents and duct tape didn't affect its capacity to hold water. In fact, it could hold water just as well as it had brand-new. I felt like God whispered, "Bethany, your wounds and sorrows haven't lessened your capacity to hold my presence. Yes, they have shaped you, made you who you are. Yet your capacity to be a carrier of my Spirit is the same." In tears, I continued to read:

O God, you are my God, earnestly I seek you;
My soul thirsts for you,
My body longs for you.

I realized then that I had been looking at capacity in the wrong way. It's not about my capacity to hold people's trauma but about my capacity to hold more of God in places and with people affected by trauma. I might not be able to do the same work I'd been doing, but I could still care for those who are suffering. Filled with God's love and strength, I can sit with people, grieve with them, and love them from a place of fullness. If I'm giving love and care out of my own capacity, then I will burn out. I don't have what it takes. I'm weak and need more of God. People aren't asking me to fix them, to carry their trauma; they're inviting me to be present, to feel and invite the presence of God, who is my healer and theirs.

I'm still very much on this journey. Even as I wrote this book, I kept forgetting to pay attention to my needs. I forgot to take bathroom breaks, to prioritize my daily practice, and to remember that I'm beloved, no matter what. I don't have this figured out.

As I mentioned earlier, our greatest burden can become the source of our greatest gift. I'm now witnessing this in my own life. The suffering I experienced through burnout has led to this book and to my passion to care for others who are affected by secondary trauma. This is part of what I get to offer to this world.

To close, I humbly offer a few grounding truths that have arisen out of my codependent brokenness, my need for God, and the gift of my belovedness:

- *I am loved, not for what I do but because I am.* My worth and value do not depend on how I am received or accepted. Nor do they depend on how effective and helpful I am to others and this world. I am loved just as I am.
- *I am not the healer; God is the Healer.* I get to point people to Jesus, yet I also witness Jesus speaking the truth in deep soul places where my words of comfort, truth, and encouragement don't reach.
- *I am not the hands and feet of God.* God works outside of me as well as through me. When I cry out to God for help, I see the impossible happen. Mountains move and challenges are overcome in ways that even the best advocacy and clinical methods can't accomplish.
- *I need to ask for help; I can't do it all.* I have limitations and that's not only completely normal but also a good thing. It's okay to say no, maybe, and tomorrow. I'm dependent on God and on others. Neither God nor other people expect me to have all the answers or to be able to figure everything out on my own.
- *I need to rest and learn to receive.* I need regular times of reflection in prayer. The pain of others penetrates me deeply, so I need to be

replenished and filled with God's presence to survive. I can be okay with unproductiveness. I can choose gratitude and receive joy.

SOME FINAL REFLECTION QUESTIONS

- What grounding truths arise for you today? How do you want to let these truths inform how you move forward?
- What small steps of change do you want to make? Remember to start small with a daily practice for the season that you are in.

The appendix includes a few exercises that have been mentioned throughout. May this be an offering for continued growth and exploration, not an overwhelming list of to-dos.

Grace upon grace. You are beloved.

Praise the Lord, my soul,
  and forget not all his benefits—
who forgives all your sins
  and heals all your diseases,
who redeems your life from the pit
  and crowns you with love and compassion,
who satisfies your desires with good things
  so that your youth is renewed like the eagle's.
    (Psalm 103:2-5 NIV)

ACKNOWLEDGMENTS

I'm incredibly grateful for friends and family who encouraged me to write this book and provided valuable feedback. Thank you, my dear husband, Kenny, for your ongoing support, including staying up late to read and edit chapters, even after a full day in med school. You amaze me. I wouldn't have submitted a book proposal let alone finished this book without your love and support. Your steadfast voice of wisdom has been (mostly) welcome and definitely transformative to my false beliefs and unhealthy habits. I'm truly a more grounded, loving person because of you.

Thank you, Mom and Dad (Tim and Kerry), for being an inspiration to love God holistically, to love others, and to love myself. Thank you for offering your valuable insight and for reading the whole manuscript three times. Thank you for affirming my voice as well as watching Acadia and Lillian so I could work. And thank you to our daughters, for your long naps and grace for my tiredness. I hope this work blesses you someday as well.

Andrea and Ali, I'm so grateful to call you sisters and to witness your pursuits of wholeness. Thank you, my other sis, Kelly, for ripping apart the intro, and Mary Ann for welcoming each chapter and providing feedback and encouragement. Thank you, Catherine (the first to read it all!), as well as Hannah, Heather, Cheri, Eileen, Kara, and Sara for your friendship, cheerleading, and editing of multiple chapters.

I'm also grateful for friends who have journeyed with me in my quest for holistic soul care. Elizabeth, yours was the first voice of grace and challenge to my codependent workaholic behavior. Thank you, Eliz, Nick, Liz, Ben, and Sara, for being community, bringing much joy, and asking thoughtful questions about my life/work balance. Your friendship and encouragement to continue to pursue this book as well as the gift of countless conversations has been a source of life and fresh air.

Thank you to my dear colleagues at Tierra Nueva over the years. I'm honored to have worked alongside each of you; you have challenged me, taught me, and encouraged me to grow. Danielle and Kevin, thank you for cheering me on with this book and offering your story. Your stunning pursuit of change and your desire to live and to love others well inspire me. Thank you, Chris, for your collaboration and humility as well as your beautiful example of seeking and offering wholehearted change. Thank you, Mike, Amy and Alan, Bob and Gracie, Salvio and Victoria, and Julio, for all that I've learned about inner healing and colaboring with God from each of you. Also thanks to Muias for your pursuit of holistic recovery and for bringing the Genesis Process training to Tierra Nueva. Anne and Claire, thank you for inviting me, a fellow wounded healer, into your own soul care and showing up with such honesty and grace. David, you've stopped me in my technology loop more than once, modeled instant Maui breaks, and along with Matt and Alvin, thanks to each of you for validating and encouraging my trauma-informed soul care interests.

Kathy and Lorie, your impact on me is evident throughout this book. Thank you for walking with me in my soul care journey. I'm filled with gratitude for your thoughtful questions, your grace and kindness, and the space you created for my inner soil to be dug up and for much to be planted.

Nancy Murphy and Northwest Family Life therapists, I'm so grateful to journey with you in trauma-informed soul care. Thank you for welcoming me into your stories, for your belief in this work, and for offering the opportunity to share what I've been learning.

Laura van Dernoot Lipsky, thank you for offering the world the wisdom you gained through your own burnout journey. Your class and book helped set a new trajectory in my life.

I wish I could also thank Henri Nouwen in person. Your emphasis of our belovedness has profoundly impacted me and continues to have a ripple effect in my life.

Finally, thank you, Ed Gilbreath and InterVarsity Press, for taking this on—believing it's worth it—for your valuable feedback, and for graciously walking with me through my blind spots. You have truly helped make this a better book.

APPENDIX ONE

GROUNDING PRACTICES

FREE-WRITE EXERCISE

To free-write means to write down everything that comes to mind. As much as possible, do this without judgment, as there are no wrong answers. Time yourself with one minute per prompt, a total of five minutes. Consider making this a daily practice.

- I feel . . .
- I fear . . .
- I am . . .
- I want . . .
- I hope . . .

DAILY PRAYER

Creating your own daily prayer can be a way to connect with God through also reminding yourself of needed truths. To begin, try free-writing based on the prompts below. Time yourself one minute each, or just let yourself write.

- Today, I ask for . . .
- I am free to . . .
- Help me, Lord, to . . .
- I give thanks for . . .
- I affirm that I am . . .

Now take what you've written and turn it into something that you want to pray each day. Perhaps consider these questions:

- What do you want to remind yourself of daily?
- What do you want to bring to God? To receive from God?

Make it your own, for this season or for life in general.

BREATH PRAYER

The following is based on *Sacred Rhythms: Arranging Our Lives for Spiritual Transformation* by Ruth Haley Barton.

- *Slowing down.* "Begin by spending time quietly in God's presence, allowing yourself to settle into that beyond-words place of comfort and intimacy, receptivity and restful repose." Breathe gently, deeply, just enough to make a candle flicker. Breathe in, breathe out.
- *Desiring.* Imagine God calling you by name and asking, "What do you want?" Free-write on the following: "God, what I most want from you right now is . . ."
- *Connecting.* What name or image of God most resonates right now? God, who do you want to be for me right now?
- *Praying.* Combine your desire with the name or quality of God that you especially need in this season, such as mercy, love, belonging, or connection. Prayer examples include:
    - Jesus, have mercy on me.
    - I am beloved.
    - Abba, I belong to you.
    - "Be still and know that I am God."

Breathe in, breathe out, praying the phrase as you do. Try incorporating it into your day. Breathe it when you are waiting in line, when you are worried, when you are in the shower, "when you need some sense of God's presence."

FIVE SENSES WALK

- Talk a walk outside. As you walk, notice your surroundings with all of your senses. What do you smell, hear, taste, feel, and see?

- Walk slowly, listening for the crunch of leaves, the smells around you, the feeling of the ground beneath you.
- Notice and experience being present with your whole body.
- As you walk back, notice how you feel in your body. How does this feeling differ from how you normally walk?

TRUST BOWL

- Find a bowl and place it where you'll notice it when you come home.
- Write the names of people you're working with or feel burdened for on small pieces of paper or stones. Place these in the bowl.
- At the end of the day, pick up each paper or stone. Lay each back down in the bowl one at a time. As you do this, bless them and be mindful of surrendering them to Jesus.

APPENDIX TWO

REFLECTIONS AND PRAYER EXERCISES

REPLACING FALSE BELIEFS

Scripture Reflection

Before praying about a false belief, spend time contemplating the Scriptures below. Are there any that stand out to you? What does Jesus want to say to you right now?

- We're created to have "the mind of Christ" (1 Corinthians 2:16).
- We're invited, even commanded, to seek God's kingdom first in our lives, in our minds, and in our whole selves. "Seek first his kingdom and his righteousness, and all these things will be given to you as well" (Matthew 6:33 NIV).
- We're encouraged to remember what God has done for us and what is good. "Finally, beloved, whatever is true, whatever is honorable, whatever is just, whatever is pure, whatever is pleasing, whatever is commendable, if there is any excellence and if there is anything worthy of praise, think about these things" (Philippians 4:8).
- We are new creations, invited to put away former ways of being and to be made new. "You were taught to put away your former way of life, your old self, corrupt and deluded by its lusts, and to be renewed in the spirit of your minds, and to clothe yourselves with the new self, created according to the likeness of God in true righteousness and holiness" (Ephesians 4:22-24).

- Jesus perceives and equates our thoughts with what is in our heart. Perhaps he considers our false beliefs evil, because they are contrary to truth. "Jesus, perceiving their thoughts, said, 'Why do you think evil in your hearts?'" (Matthew 9:4).
- We have authority and power to take "every thought captive to obey Christ" (2 Corinthians 10:5).

Prayer Exercise

- *Centering*. Welcome God in your midst. Perhaps pray through a breath prayer, the Welcoming Prayer, or your daily prayer to let go of what you might be carrying and to receive what God has for you in this time.
- *Naming*. Write down negative thoughts about yourself that have recently surfaced. Invite God to show you which one to focus on for this prayer time.
- *Confessing*. Speak out and confess your belief. Let yourself hear it out loud. How does it feel to say it? Where do you feel it in your body? Where does it weigh on you? What toll has it taken on you?
- *Forgiving*. Ask for forgiveness for believing the negative belief. It's contrary to how God sees you and invites you to live. Also ask God to show you who has contributed to this belief. Did you receive it from parents/caregivers? How has your culture/community impacted this belief? When ready, forgive those who have contributed to forming the false belief.
- *Receiving*. Receive God's forgiveness for believing it, and extend that forgiveness toward yourself and others.
- *Renouncing*. Break your agreement with the belief. Speak out your desire to be rid of it.

- *Replacing*. Invite God to replace the false belief with what is true. If you have a hard time hearing what is true, invite others to speak into your life, or go to Scripture.
- *Living*. Write down what you sense or hear God is saying to you. Let yourself experience God's love and grace to you. What else do you need to live into this new truth? Invite God's presence into the places where you've carried it in your body and the areas of your life that it has affected. Consider what practical changes you might need to make.

Are you tired? Worn out? Burned out on religion? Come to me. Get away with me and you'll recover your life. I'll show you how to take a real rest. Walk with me and work with me—watch how I do it. Learn the unforced rhythms of grace. I won't lay anything heavy or ill-fitting on you. Keep company with me and you'll learn to live freely and lightly.

MATTHEW 11: 28-30 (MSG)

MOVING BEYOND CODEPENDENCY

Sometimes we give up on people, judge them, or appease them because of *our* desire for *their* change. If you want someone to change, consider why that is. How does it make you feel? How does it affect you to see people suffering and make harmful choices? When you don't understand others' choices, try putting on compassionate investigative lenses and seek to understand them. Do they not text back because of shame, fear of failing, or disappointing you? Do they have a hard time asking for help?

- *Naming*. Ask Jesus to bring to mind someone with whom it's challenging to maintain healthy boundaries, who you are seeking to "help," or who's pressing your buttons. How does their behavior affect you? What is contributing to those challenges? What buttons do they press in you?

- *Inviting Jesus' perspective.* What does Jesus see is going on with them? How does Jesus see them? What is Jesus doing or want to be doing?
- *Considering your role and needs.* How does Jesus see your role? What do you need to let go of? What do you need to receive? What need do you have that is not getting met? How can you meet and communicate those needs? Remember, if you have a need to be affirmed, to be respected, to have agency, those are normal and healthy needs.
- *Extend compassion.* What does it look like to have compassion on yourself? What might it look like to have compassion on this person?
- *Invite Jesus to lead you in how to respond.* What is the remedy? What do you need to communicate to this person? What support do you need in order to do that?

SURRENDERING BURDENS

(Based on Burden Bearing Prayer Exercise developed by Lorie Martin and Eden Jersak.)

> *Take my yoke upon you, . . . for my yoke is easy, and my burden is light.*
> MATTHEW 11:30 (NIV)

Centering. Read the beginning of Psalm 23, and imagine yourself there with Jesus. Brad Jersak calls this creating a "Meeting Place" (for more guidance, see his *Can You Hear Me?: Tuning in to the God who Speaks*, Monarch Books, 2006). After centering in that place, notice where Jesus is and what he is doing and saying. Start asking him questions, such as the following ones.

Naming the burden. We are often carrying burdens, feeling weighed down by things in our lives, by stress and anxiety. What do you feel weighed down by?

- What burden does Jesus want to lift of you right now?
- What does the burden look like? If it were an object what would it be?

Identifying the cost and benefit. Where do you carry this burden? What does it cost you to carry this burden?

- What's the payoff of keeping it? Any reason you need to keep carrying it?
- Is there anything that prevents you from giving this burden to Jesus?

Surrendering the burden.

- What would Jesus like to do with the burden?
- What do you want to do with it? Throw it on the ground? Safely entrust it to Jesus' caring and capable hands?
- Are you willing to give it to him? If you are, open your hands, picture the object or burden, and then empty your hands, seeing what Jesus does with the burden.

Receiving the gift.

- What gift does Jesus want to give you in its place? Open your hands and receive whatever gift Jesus wants to give you in its place.

THE GARDEN WALL

Healthy boundaries are like a garden wall or a property line. I can look and reach over the wall, but the wall is present. It isn't a barricade between me and others. There is a well-functioning gate that I can open and close. I can choose who I invite into my garden. I can invite them, and I can say no to someone entering. Dr. Henry Cloud and Dr. John Townsend write, "The owner of the property is legally responsible for what happens on his or her property. Non-owners are not responsible for the property."

With ownership of our garden or property comes responsibility to tend to and to care for it. A property line defines where someone's property ends and where someone else's begins.

Engage with this image of your life as a garden. You might do this silently, through journaling, or by drawing. Invite Jesus to show you what your garden wall looks like.

- How high is it?
- What is it made of?
- Does it need to be repaired? Where and with what?
- What's in the garden?
- Why does it need to be protected?
- Is there someone within the garden wall who needs to be asked to leave?
- Where is Jesus, and what is he doing?

Imagine yourself in the garden, relaxing, making yourself at home. Spend time there as a part of a daily practice.

GUIDELINE FOR LIVING

(Based on Ruth Haley Barton's Rule of Life in *Sacred Rhythms* and Cheryl Richardson's *The Art of Extreme Self-Care.*)

First Draft: Writing a Guideline for Living

- Spend time with the reflection questions at the end of chapter thirteen. "Acknowledge the mystery of spiritual transformation and powerlessness to bring it about on your own."

- Write a first draft of the "Identifying Rhythms of Rest" questions below. Take a break, and come back to the plan a few weeks later.
- Consider what changes you might need to make in your schedule in order to choose this guideline.
- Invite support and accountability by showing your plan to a friend or your partner, welcoming that person's input and support.
- Commit yourself with grace, prayerfully. Check in six months later, notice how it's going. Be gentle with yourself.

Identifying Rhythms of Rest

- *Daily.* What practices will I seek to engage in on a daily basis? What practices would be life-giving during the morning, midday, and evening?
- *In transition.* What will help me to let go of the day's events? What would help recenter me after an intense appointment or when arriving home from work?
- *Weekly.* What activities bring me joy? What activities take away joy? Consider this exhortation from Ruth Haley Brown: "What activities . . . will I refuse to engage in so that [my sabbath] is truly a day of rest, worship and delight?"
- *Monthly, quarterly, or yearly.* What space would be helpful to set aside as a monthly, quarterly, or yearly time of reflection and rest? What is feasible for this year?

NOTES

INTRODUCTION: CONFESSIONS OF A SOCIAL JUSTICE WORKAHOLIC

4 *Psychologists call this secondary trauma*: Beth Hudnall Stamm, "Professional Quality of Life and Secondary Traumatic Stress," *ProQOL Manual,* accessed February 1, 2018, www.proqol.org/Secondary_Trauma.html.

7 *Go slow / if you can*: Jan Richardson, "A Blessing for Traveling in the Dark," © Jan Richardson from *Circle of Grace: A Book of Blessings for the Seasons* (Orlando, FL: Wanton Gospeller Press, 2015), janrichardson.com. Used with permission.

1. TRAUMA-INFORMED SOUL CARE

13 *A person gets overly*: Christina Maslach, *Burnout: The Cost of Caring* (Englewood Cliffs, NJ: Prentice-Hall, 1982), 3.

detached, callous and even: Maslach, *Burnout,* 4.

15 *Denial of our authentic*: Sayu Bhojwani, "Let's Get Real About Why Women of Color Are So Tired," *ZORA*, Medium, February 11, 2020, zora.medium.com/lets-get-real-about-why-women-of-color-are-so-tired-fe3966f1b510.

Exposure to continuous racism: Jasmine Brown, "Self-Care for People of Color After Psychological Trauma," *Just Jasmine*, July 5, 2016, justjasmineblog.com/blog-1/self-care-for-people-of-color-after-emotional-and-psychological-trauma/.

16 *The ability to descend*: See Sheila Wise Rowe, *Healing Racial Trauma: The Road to Resilience* (Downers Grove, IL: InterVarsity Press, 2020); W. Cross, "Black Psychological Functioning and the Legacy of Slavery," in Y. Danieli, ed., *The International Handbook of Multigenerational Legacies of Trauma* (New York: Plenum Press, 1998); P. Elsass, "Individual and Collective Traumatic Memories: A Qualitative Study of PTSD Symptoms in Two Latin American Localities," *Transcultural Psychiatry* 38, no. 3 (2001): 306-16.

[Fifteen hundred] pastors leave: Kevin Halloran, "Christian Ministry Burnout: Prevention, Signs, Statistics, and Recovery," *Leadership Resources*, October 22, 2013, www.leadershipresources.org/blog/christian-ministry-burnout-prevention-signs-statistics-recovery/.

17 *Many social workers would*: In the study "Self-care and Professional Quality of Life," done among MSW practitioners, researchers found that "while social workers value and believe self-care is effective in alleviating job-related stress, they engage in self-care on a limited basis." Kori R. Bloomquist, et al., "Self-care and Professional Quality of Life: Predictive Factors Among MSW Practitioners," *Advances in Social Work* 16, no. 2 (Fall 2015), 292, https://doi.org/10.18060/18760.

19 *Self-care that engages*: The "Self-Care and Professional Quality of Life" report concluded that "very little is known about the realm of spiritual self-care among human service professionals, especially social workers. Further exploration of this domain of self-care practice is needed." Bloomquist, et al., "Self-care and Professional," 304.

20 *Not only can we become afraid*: David Whyte, *The Three Marriages* (New York: Riverhead Books, 2009), 33.

When we start asking: Whyte, *Three Marriages*, 98.

the soul is nonmaterial: David G. Benner, *Care of Souls: Revisioning Christian Nurture and Counsel* (Grand Rapids, MI: Baker Books, 1998), preface.

21 *The Hebrew understanding*: Benner, *Care of Souls,* 52-53, 63.

22 *Centering Prayer as a daily practice*: For more information on Centering Prayer, see chapter thirteen in this book as well as Contemplative Outreach's "The Method of

Centering Prayer," www.contemplativeoutreach.org/wp-content/uploads/2012/04 /method_cp_eng-2016-06_0.pdf.

22 *soul force, a philosophy of nonviolence*: Soul force was developed by Mahatma Gandhi and expanded by Martin Luther King Jr.

Soul force creates an outward: Reesheda Graham-Washington and Shawn Casselberry, *Soul Force: Seven Pivots Toward Courage, Community, and Change* (Harrisonburg, VA: Herald Press, 2018), 16.

Rooted and held: Throughout his writing, Henri Nouwen referred to a movement from solitude to community to ministry. For example, see his "Moving from Solitude to Community to Ministry," *Leadership Magazine*, Spring 1995, https://www.christianitytoday.com/pastors/1995/spring/51280.html.

Holistic, trauma-informed soul: Psych Central states, "A person with good resilience has the ability to bounce back more quickly and with less stress than someone whose resilience is less developed." "What is Resilience?" *Psych Central*, accessed October 22, 2018, psychcentral.com/lib/what-is-resilience/.

23 *While resilience helps us*: Rick Hanson and Forrest Hanson, *Resilient: How to Grow an Unshakable Core of Calm, Strength, and Happiness* (New York: Harmony Books, 2018), 2.

Laura van Dernoot Lipsky invites: Laura D. Lipsky and Connie Burk, *Trauma Stewardship: An Everyday Guide to Caring for Self While Caring for Others* (San Francisco: Berrett-Koehler Publishers, 2009), 180.

26 *Take some time*: See "Stress Symptoms" under "Articles on Stress Management," webMD, www.webmd.com/balance/stress-management/stress-symptoms-effects_of-stress-on-the-body#1.

2. LIVING AS BELOVED

28 *What's wrong with me?*: Lorie Martin, *Invited: Simple Prayer Exercises for Solitude and Community* (Abbotsford, BC: Fresh Wind Press, 2010), 128.

30 *Original blessing reminds us*: Danielle Shroyer, *Original Blessing: Putting Sin in Its Rightful Place* (Minneapolis: Fortress Press, 2016), xi.

The good news is not: The theme of original goodness is also compellingly developed in Archbishop Desmond Tutu and Mpho Tutu's book *Made for Goodness.*

Countless other messages pervade: Shroyer, *Original Blessing*, x.

31 *What we do doesn't give*: Shroyer, *Original Blessing*, 10.

32 *For six years, I led*: Dialogical Bible study involves reading Scripture with people through asking questions and contextualizing the stories based on people's lived experiences. To learn more, read Bob Ekblad's *Reading the Bible with the Damned* and Gerald West's *The Academy of the Poor: Towards a Dialogical Reading of the Bible.*

33 *There is no need to plead*: Amy Carmichael, *If: What Do I Know of Calvary Love?* (New York: Popular Classics Publishing, 2012), 20-21.

35 *Prison Contemplative Fellowship*: See www.uspcf.org.

Contemplative Outreach: See www.contemplativeoutreach.org.

"Becoming the Beloved": Graham Cooke, *Becoming the Beloved*, www.youtube.com /watch?v=XOeQjMJVZRk&list=PLY-__l5XSfglGVufCye1OViXXmN3xppAh.

"Laughter Came From Every Brick": St. Teresa of Avila, "Laughter Came From Every Brick" in Daniel Ladinsky, *Love Poems from God: Twelve Sacred Voices of the East and West* (New York: Penguin Random House, 2002), 276. Used with permission.

3. WOUNDED HEALERS

39 *personal trauma motivates the majority*: A. Barr, "An Investigation into the extent to which Psychological Wounds Inspire Counsellors and Psychotherapists to become Wounded

Healers, the Significance of These Wounds on Their Career Choice, the Causes of These Wounds and the Overall Significance of Demographic Factors," *The Green Rooms,* 2006, accessed February 15, 2020, www.thegreenrooms.net/wounded-healer/.

39 *asking for healing and help*: Danielle Shroyer, *Original Blessing: Putting Sin In Its Rightful Place* (Minneapolis: Fortress Press, 2016), 170.

40 *Like an infection*: Shroyer, *Original Blessing*, 170.

Jesus, who makes his: Henri Nouwen, *The Wounded Healer* (New York: Doubleday, 1979), 82-83.

What I have to give to others: David. G. Benner, *Care of Souls: Revisioning Christian Nurture and Counsel* (Grand Rapids, MI: Baker Books, 1998), 150-51.

41 *In contrast, if we don't*: Benner, *Care of Souls,* 150-51.

Facing these deep truths: David Benner, *The Gift of Being Yourself: The Sacred Call to Self-Discovery* (Downers Grove, IL: InterVarsity Press, 2004), 72.

4. SECONDARY TRAUMA

47 *In a similar way*: Judith Herman, *Trauma and Recovery: The Aftermath of Violence—From Domestic Abuse to Political Terror* (New York: Basic Books, 1997), 141.

48 *Even just hearing about trauma*: Françoise Mathieu, *The Compassion Fatigue Workbook: Creative Tools for Transforming Compassion Fatigue and Vicarious Traumatization* (New York: Routledge, 2015), 14.

microaggression is: Sheila Wise Rowe, *Healing Racial Trauma: The Road to Resilience* (Downers Grove, IL: InterVarsity Press, 2020), 15.

Abuse accurately describes: Ibram X. Kendi, *How to be an Antiracist* (New York: Random House, 2019) 47.

I was anxious: Rowe, *Healing Racial Trauma*, 14.

49 *Trauma affects our capacity*: Serene Jones, *Trauma and Grace: Theology in a Ruptured World* (Louisville, KY: Westminster John Knox, 2009), 29.

They override your powers: Jones, *Trauma and Grace*, 29.

self-esteem is assaulted: Herman, *Trauma and Recovery*, 56.

if we think we're struggling: Christina Maslach, *Burnout: The Cost of Caring* (Englewood Cliffs, NJ: Prentice-Hall, 1982), 11.

50 *syndrome of emotional exhaustion*: See Christina Maslach, et al., "Maslach Burnout Inventory," www.mindgarden.com/117-maslach-burnout-inventory.

It's a response to the: Maslach, *Burnout*, 3.

It's work to be the only: Austin Channing Brown, *I'm Still Here: Black Dignity in a World Made for Whiteness* (New York: Convergent Books, 2018), 21.

Moral injury is: "What is Moral Injury?" Syracuse University Moral Injury Project, http://moralinjuryproject.syr.edu/about-moral-injury/.

51 *It arises from the challenge*: Rowe, *Healing Racial Trauma*, 17.

Due to moral injury: Simon G. and Wendy Dean Talbot, "Physicians Are Not Burning Out—They Are Suffering Moral Injury," First Opinion, *STAT News,* July 26, 2018, statnews.com/2018/07/26/physicians-not-burning-out-they-are-suffering-moral-injury/.

52 *having tar dry*: Brown, *I'm Still Here*, 107.

Lipsky rightly calls guilt: Laura van Dernoot Lipsky, "Self Care for Social Workers," University of Washington School of Social Work Class, Spring 2010.

53 *sense that one can never*: Laura D. Lipsky and Connie Burk, *Trauma Stewardship: An Everyday Guide to Caring for Self While Caring for Others* (San Francisco: Berrett-Koehler Publishers, 2009), 95.

53 *never do enough*: Lipsky, *Trauma Stewardship*, 59.

54 *secondary trauma exposure*: See Lipsky and Burk's *Trauma Stewardship* for more examples of trauma exposure.

This is an assessment: Beth Hudnall Stamm, "Professional Quality of Life Measure: Compassion Satisfaction," ProQOL, accessed February 1, 2018, proqol.org/Compassion_Satisfaction.html.

5. CODEPENDENCY IN THE WORKPLACE

58 *codependency is more common*: Melody Beattie, *Codependent No More: How to Stop Controlling Others and Start Caring for Yourself* (Center City, MN: Hazelden, 1992), 33.

59 *I've come to trust the value*: Gregory Boyle, *Tattoos on the Heart* (New York: Free Press, 2010), 127.

In my early, crazy days: Boyle, *Tattoos*, 125.

60 *I found consolation*: Boyle, *Tattoos,* 5.

As a defense against: Judith Herman, *Trauma and Recovery: The Aftermath of Violence—From Domestic Abuse to Political Terror* (New York: Basic Books, 1997), 142.

Human love is directed: Dietrich Bonhoeffer, *Life Together* (San Francisco: HarperSanFrancisco, 2008), 33-35.

61 *In contrast, codependents who*: Co-Dependents Anonymous International, "Recovery Patterns of Co-Dependence," Co-Dependence Anonymous, Inc., accessed September 28, 2018, coda.org/default/assets/File/Foundational%20Documents/2011%20Patterns%20of%20Recovery%20%202015.pdf.

These are often the hardest: Richard Rohr, *Breathing Under Water: Spirituality and the Twelve Steps* (Cincinnati, OH: St. Anthony Messenger Press, 2011), xxiii.

She continued by writing: Brené Brown, *Rising Strong* (New York: Spiegel and Grau, 2015), 63-64.

62 *We pick up not only another*: Bessel van der Kolk, *The Body Keeps the Score: Brain, Mind, and Body in the Healing of Trauma* (New York: Penguin Books, 2014), 59.

63 *empathy is*: David. G. Benner, *Care of Souls: Revisioning Christian Nurture and Counsel* (Grand Rapids, MI: Baker Books, 1998), 139.

Being in recovery is being: Co-Dependents Anonymous International, "Recovery Patterns of Co-Dependence."

64 *personality types who are attracted*: Françoise Mathieu, *The Compassion Fatigue Workbook: Creative Tools for Transforming Compassion Fatigue and Vicarious Traumatization* (New York: Routledge, 2015), 22.

The survivor who is often: Herman, *Trauma and Recovery*, 61.

65 *the "you" that God loves*: Lorie Martin, *Invited: Simple Prayer Exercises for Solitude and Community* (Abbotsford, BC: Fresh Wind Press, 2010), 49.

Attend a Co-Dependents Anonymous: Visit Co-Dependents Anonymous International at www.coda.org.

66 *Poem by Heather Tillery*: Heather Tillery, "When I Learn," unpublished poem. Used with permission.

6. NEEDS AND DESIRES

67 *After my conversion, I became*: Jack Frost, "When My Old Demons Crept Back In, God's Love Saved Me and My Entire Family!," Destiny Image, March 15, 2019, destinyimage.com/2019/03/15/jack-frost-my-experience-with-fathers-embrace/.

68 *the more we prayed*: Frost, "When My Old Demons."

question to continually ask ourselves is: Laura D Lipsky and Connie Burk, *Trauma*

Stewardship: An Everyday Guide to Caring for Self While Caring for Others (San Francisco: Berrett-Koehler Publishers, 2009), 147.

69 *Yet our human need for*: Contemplative Outreach, *Welcoming Prayer: Consent on the Go, a 40-Day Praxis* (West Milford, NJ: Contemplative Outreach, LTD, 2018), 9. Used with permission.

70 *safety, satisfaction, and connection*: Judith Herman, *Trauma and Recovery: The Aftermath of Violence—From Domestic Abuse to Political Terror* (New York: Basic Books, 1997), 3.

The creator of NVC: Jack Frost, *Experiencing Father's Embrace* (Shippensburg, PA: Destiny Image, 2006), 53-54.

We develop patterns of behavior: Cherry Haisten, "The Practice of Welcoming Prayer," Contemplative Outreach, Ltd., accessed February 15, 2019, www.contemplativeoutreach.org/wp-content/uploads/2018/02/practiceofthewelcomingprayer_0.pdf.

71 *Referencing the story of the prodigal*: Frost, *Experiencing Father's Embrace*, 87.

the myth of heroic sacrifice: Richard Rohr, *Breathing Under Water: Spirituality and the Twelve Steps* (Cincinnati, OH: St. Anthony Messenger Press, 2011), 21.

In doing so, we deny: Bill Johnson, *Dreaming with God* (Shippensburg, PA: Destiny Image, 2006), 31.

72 *Such questions had the power*: Ruth Haley Barton, *Sacred Rhythms: Arranging Our Lives for Spiritual Transformation* (Downers Grove, IL: InterVarsity Press, 2006), 23.

What good is it: Laura van Dernoot Lipsky, "Self Care for Social Workers," University of Washington School of Social Work class, Spring 2010.

should enhance the lives of others: Desmond and Mpho Tutu, *Made for Goodness: And Why this Makes All the Difference* (New York: HarperCollins, 2010), 47.

73 *lays the groundwork for reconciliation*: John Perkins and Karen Waddles, *One Blood: Parting Words to the Church on Race* (Chicago: Moody, 2018), 21.

Even still, he offers his: Perkins and Waddles, *One Blood,* 80.

75 *We're also more aware*: Paraphrased from Barton, *Sacred Rhythms*, 17, 24.

Marshall Rosenberg's Nonviolent Communication: Marshall Rosenberg, "Needs Inventory," Center for Nonviolent Communication, cnvc.org/Training/needs-inventory.

autonomy, celebration, integrity: Marshall B. Rosenberg, *Nonviolent Communication* (Encinitas, CA: PuddleDancer Press, 2002), 210.

7. FALSE BELIEFS

77 *One barrier to taking care*: Other barriers participants mention include time, energy, finances, lack of familial modeling of self-care, and a history of experiencing oppression.

78 *The fact that our beliefs*: Michael Dye and Patricia Fancher, *The Genesis Process: A Relapse Prevention Workbook for Addictive/Compulsive Behaviors,* 3rd ed. (Auburn, CA: Genesis Addiction Process, 2007), 36. Material from the Genesis Process used throughout this book is used with permission.

what is broken: Michael Dye, "Genesis Process: A New Beginning," 2018, accessed April 23, 2018, genesisprocess.org.

a symbol only of injustice: Brenda Salter McNeil and Rick Richardson, *The Heart of Racial Justice: How Soul Change Leads to Social Change* (Downers Grove, IL: InterVarsity Press, 2004), 83.

79 *hip white person identity*: McNeil, *Racial Justice*, 83.

experts swoop in with their answers: Ryan Kuja, "6 Harmful Consequences of the

White Savior Complex," *Sojourners*, July 24, 2019, sojo.net/articles/6-harmful-consequences-white-savior-complex.

79 *The White Savior Complex*: Kuja, "6 Harmful Consequences."

80 *we not only have successes*: Henri Nouwen, *Out of Solitude: Three Meditations on the Christian Life* (Notre Dame: Ave Maria Press, 1983), 18.

According to the Genesis Process: Genesis Process, "Relapse Prevention," accessed September 9, 2017, www.genesisprocess.org/relapse-prevention/.

81 *trust is foolish*: Dr. Dan B. Allender, *The Wounded Heart: Hope for Adult Victims of Childhood Sexual Abuse* (Colorado Springs, CO: NavPress, 2014), 25.

From the moment we: Restoring the Foundations, "Our God is a God of Truth," 2016, accessed April 24, 2018, restoringthefoundations.org/integrated-approach.

Every day we all: McNeil, *Racial Justice*, 74.

If you have a model-minority: McNeil, *Racial Justice*, 83.

82 *We must admit*: McNeil, *Racial Justice*, 79.

To be wholesome: John O'Donohue, *Anam Cara: A Book of Celtic Wisdom* (New York: HarperCollins, 1997), xvi.

8. IDENTIFYING STAGES OF CHANGE

89 *Circumstances placed drugs*: Danielle Riley, "Thoughts on Relapse," unpublished notes, September 24, 2019.

Transtheoretical Model: James O. Prochaska and Carlo C. DiClemente, "The Transtheoretical Approach," in John C. Norcross and Marvin R. Goldfried, eds., *Handbook of Psychotherapy Integration*, 2nd ed., Oxford Series in Clinical Psychology (New York: Oxford University Press, 2005), 147-71.

91 *The National Institute for Drug Abuse states*: National Institute for Drug Abuse, "Drugs, Brains, and Behavior: The Science of Addiction," July 1, 2014, drugabuse.gov/publications/drugs-brains-behavior-science-addiction.

The whole first year: Kevin Riley, interview about relapse, September 19, 2019.

92 *Knowing what to do*: Michael Dye and Patricia Fancher, *The Genesis Process: A Relapse Prevention Workbook for Addictive/Compulsive Behaviors*, 3rd ed. (Auburn, CA: Genesis Addiction Process, 2007), 72.

FASTER is an acronym: For the full FASTER Scale description, see the handouts on the Genesis Process website, genesisprocess.org/handouts/.

Negative emotions are often: Dye and Fancher, *Genesis Process,* 73.

94 *They may have received*: Bruce Demarest, *Soul Guide: Following Jesus as Spiritual Director* (Colorado Springs, CO: NavPress, 2003), 31-32.

Often in this third stage: Demarest, *Soul Guide,* 32.

Persuaded that the old pattern: Demarest, *Soul Guide,* 32.

Danielle said she was able: Danielle Riley, "Thoughts on Relapse."

95 *The call may be to the same*: Demarest, *Soul Guide,* 32.

Danielle and Kevin Riley's podcast: See holdfastpodcast.org.

9. MOVING FROM SHAME TO SELF-EMPATHY

98 *Shame is the feeling*: Brené Brown, *Dare to Lead* (New York: Random House, 2018), 75.

99 *The Genesis Process Counselors Manual*: Michael Dye, *The Genesis Process Counselors Manual* (Auburn, CA: Genesis Addiction Process, 2008), 55.

This is largely because of the belief: Dye, *Counselors Manual*, 55.

100 *Emotional intelligence is*: *Oxford Living Dictionary,* s.v. "emotional intelligence," en.oxforddictionaries.com/definition/emotional_intelligence.

101 *We neglect the need*: John Perkins and Karen Waddles, *One Blood: Parting Words to the Church on Race* (Chicago: Moody, 2018), 68.

In his encouragement: Perkins, *One Blood*, 67.

Although much more can: See Sheila Wise Rowe's *Healing Racial Trauma* and Walter Brueggemann's *The Prophetic Imagination.*

Judith Herman emphasizes: Judith Herman, *Trauma and Recovery: The Aftermath of Violence—From Domestic Abuse to Political Terror* (New York: Basic Books, 1997), 3.

102 *According to Contemplative Outreach*: Contemplative Outreach, "Welcoming Prayer Tri-fold," Contemplative Outreach, accessed January 8, 2019, contemplativeoutreach.org/sites/default/files/private/welcoming_prayer_trifold_2016.pdf. Used with permission.

Using your intuitive eye: Contemplative Outreach, *Welcoming Prayer: Consent on the Go, a 40-Day Praxis* (West Milford, NJ: Contemplative Outreach, LTD, 2018), 23. Used with permission.

103 *When I'm moving fast*: The S in the Genesis Process's acronym FASTER stands for "speeding up."

We end up turning to: Bessel van der Kolk, *The Body Keeps the Score: Brain, Mind, and Body in the Healing of Trauma* (New York: Penguin, 2014), 99.

It's too easy, as: Brown, *Rising Strong* (New York: Spiegel and Grau, 2015), 49.

Brown echoes the importance: Brown, *Rising Strong*, 46.

104 *We let the feeling be*: Contemplative Outreach, *Welcoming Prayer*, 32.

[Welcoming Prayer] embraces: Contemplative Outreach, "Welcoming Prayer Tri-fold."

Contemplative Outreach encourages letting: Contemplative Outreach, "Welcoming Prayer Tri-fold."

105 *Practicing self-empathy*: See Cheryl Richardson, *The Art of Extreme Self-Care: Transform Your Life One Month at a Time* (Carlsbad, CA: Hay House, 2009), 5.

emergency first-aid: Marshall B. Rosenberg, *Nonviolent Communication* (Encinitas, CA: PuddleDancer Press, 2003), 103.

10. EMBRACING OUR NEED FOR OTHERS

110 *Pride is the number-one enemy*: Michael Dye and Patricia Fancher, *The Genesis Process: A Relapse Prevention Workbook for Addictive/Compulsive Behaviors*, 3rd ed. (Auburn, CA: Genesis Addiction Process, 2007), 130.

111 *What all of these examples*: Cheryl Richardson, *The Art of Extreme Self-Care: Transform Your Life One Month at a Time* (Carlsbad, CA: Hay House, 2009), 34-35.

When you judge yourself: Brené Brown, *Rising Strong* (New York: Spiegel and Grau, 2015), 180.

112 *Recovery can take place*: Judith Herman, *Trauma and Recovery: The Aftermath of Violence—From Domestic Abuse to Political Terror* (New York: Basic Books, 1997), 133, 141, 151.

This is not systemic change: Sayu Bhojwani, "Let's Get Real About Why Women of Color Are So Tired," *ZORA,* Medium, February 11, 2020, zora.medium.com/lets-get-real-about-why-women-of-color-are-so-tired-fe3966f1b510.

most powerful protection: Bessel van der Kolk, *The Body Keeps the Score: Brain, Mind, and Body in the Healing of Trauma* (New York: Penguin, 2014), 81.

113 *supportive relationships*: "Resilience: Social Support and Relationships," *Headington Institute,* accessed October 23, 2018, headington-institute.org/topic-areas/123/resilience/130/social-support-and-relationships.

A balanced recovery plan: Dye and Fancher, *The Genesis Process*, 130.

11. CHANGING BELIEFS AND BEHAVIORS

117 *We're invited to put away*: For more passages of Scripture, see "Replacing False Beliefs" in appendix two.

118 *This is called limbic lag*: Michael Dye and Patricia Fancher, *The Genesis Process: A Relapse Prevention Workbook for Addictive/Compulsive Behaviors,* 3rd ed. (Auburn, CA: Genesis Addiction Process, 2007), 68.

This includes how to walk: Curt Thompson, *Anatomy of the Soul: Surprising Connections Between Neuroscience and Spiritual Practices That Can Transform Your Life and Relationships* (Carol Stream, IL: Tyndale House, 2010), 68.

The good news is: Thompson, *Anatomy of the Soul*, 73.

Even the simple act of telling: Thompson, *Anatomy of the Soul*, 78.

119 *van der Kolk's work*: Bessel van der Kolk, *The Body Keeps the Score: Brain, Mind, and the Body in the Healing of Trauma* (New York: Penguin, 2014).

How does the false belief: The following is based on Michael Dye, *The Genesis Process: For Change Groups* (Auburn, CA: Genesis Addiction Process, 2005).

in order to engage in successful: Dye, *The Genesis Process*.

120 *All compulsive and self-destructive*: Dye, *The Genesis Process*, 45.

We need the very thing: Dye, *Change Groups*, 45.

Think: A year from: Dye, *Change Groups,* appendix.

122 *ways to slow down and self-regulate*: Even noticing these sensations and practicing breathing can be distressing for people who have experienced trauma. This is a process that must be facilitated with care. Van der Kolk, *The Body Keeps the Score*, 103.

123 *white-knuckling*: Aundie Kolber, *Try Softer: A Fresh Approach to Move Us out of Anxiety, Stress, and Survival Mode—And into a Life of Connection and Joy* (Carol Stream, IL: Tyndale House, 2020), 19.

embrace our true selves: Brenda Salter McNeil and Rick Richardson, *The Heart of Racial Justice: How Soul Change Leads to Social Change* (Downers Grove, IL: InterVarsity Press, 2004), 79.

We declare them to be: McNeil, *Racial Justice*, 79.

124 *I will make sure this pain*: Carlos Rodriguez, "Jesus, Me and the White Supremacy of American Christianity," Happy Sonship, February 11, 2018, www.happysonship.com/white-supremacy/.

Forgiveness releases us: John Perkins and Karen Waddles, *One Blood: Parting Words to the Church on Race* (Chicago: Moody, 2018), 108.

12. DISCERNING WHEN TO SAY NO AND WHEN TO SAY YES

132 *Greg McKeown leads trainings*: Greg McKeown's understanding of *essentialism* includes us choosing what's essential to do in our lives and in our work. This is different from the definition of *essentialism* that implies who we are is determined by our gender, race, etc.

nonessentialists: Greg McKeown, *Essentialism: The Disciplined Pursuit of Less* (New York: Crown Business, 2014), 166.

What boundaries do I need: Brené Brown, *Rising Strong* (New York: Spiegel and Grau, 2015), 123.

135 *a common trauma exposure response*: Laura D Lipsky and Connie Burk, *Trauma Stewardship: An Everyday Guide to Caring for Self While Caring for Others* (San Francisco: Berrett-Koehler Publishers, 2009), 70.

139 *Repairing the world*: Danielle Shroyer, *Original Blessing: Putting Sin In Its Rightful Place* (Minneapolis: Fortress Press, 2016), 146.

13. CREATING RHYTHMS OF REST AND RENEWAL

142 *marinate in the intimacy*: Gregory Boyle, *Tattoos on the Heart* (New York: Free Press, 2010), 22.

143 *Before you let the world in*: Lin-Manuel Miranda, *Gmorning, Gnight! Little Pep Talks for Me & You* (New York: Random House, 2018), 14-15.

Spirituality influences how we react: Zelana Montminy, *21 Days to Resilience: How to Transcend the Daily Grind, Deal with the Tough Stuff, and Discover Your Strongest Stuff* (New York: HarperOne, 2016), 107.

She cites various studies: Montminy, *21 Days to Resilience*, 108.

144 *We discover that being*: Henri Nouwen, *Out of Solitude: Three Meditations on the Christian Life* (Notre Dame, IN: Ave Maria Press, 1983), 22, 26.

145 *The busier we are*: Thomas Keating, *Open Mind, Open Heart: The Contemplative Dimension of the Gospel* (Rockport, MA: Element Publishing, 1991), 64.

We're often able to do: Keating, *Open Mind*, 85.

For centuries Black women: Shanesha Brooks-Tatum, "Subversive Self-Care: Centering Black Women's Wellness," *Feminist Wire*, November 9 2012, thefeministwire.com/2012/11/subversive-self-care-centering-black-womens-wellness/.

While living in Haiti: Gerard Thomas Straub, *Hidden in the Rubble: A Haitian Pilgrimage to Compassion and Resurrection* (Maryknoll, NY: Orbis, 2010), 12.

146 *There are times in my work*: Straub, *Hidden in the Rubble*, 37-38.

An emerging body of research: David DeSteno, "What Science Can Learn from Religion," *New York Times*, February 1, 2019, nytimes.com/2019/02/01/opinion/sunday/science-religion.html.

A practice is not just: Laura D. Lipsky and Connie Burk, *Trauma Stewardship: An Everyday Guide to Caring for Self While Caring for Others* (San Francisco: Berrett-Koehler Publishers, 2009), 230.

In recent years, I've been: For a concise description, see contemplativeoutreach.org/sites/default/files/documents/lectio_divina.pdf.

147 *focused attention exercises*: Curt Thompson, *Anatomy of the Soul: Surprising Connections Between Neuroscience and Spiritual Practices That Can Transform Your Life and Relationships* (Carol Stream, IL: Tyndale House, 2010), 47.

Stillness can renew: Christine Valters Paintner and Lucy Wynkoop, *Lectio Divina: Contemplative Awakening and Awareness* (New York: Paulist Press, 2008), 19.

148 *extra space between that area*: Greg McKeown, *Essentialism: The Disciplined Pursuit of Less* (New York: Crown Business, 2014), 176.

149 *Transition Times*: Lorie Martin, *Invited: Simple Prayer Exercises for Solitude and Community* (Abbotsford, BC: Fresh Wind Press, 2010), 48.

150 *Ignatius believed that God*: Kevin O'Brien, *The Ignatian Adventure: Experiencing the Ignatian Spiritual Exercises in Everyday Life* (Chicago: Loyola Press, 2011), 76-77.

As we were talking: Rosemary Crawford, *Saturated Sponge,* unpublished reflection, July 20, 2019.

152 *This is a grandiosity*: Ruth Haley Barton, *Sacred Rhythms: Arranging Our Lives for Spiritual Transformation* (Downers Grove, IL: InterVarsity Press, 2006), 138.

154 *Will this be*: Dan B. Allender, *Sabbath* (Nashville, TN: Thomas Nelson, 2009), 47.

We enter delight: Allender, *Sabbath*, 4.

155 *Sabbath is day of delight*: Allender, *Sabbath*, 5.

The way of mammon: Walter Brueggemann, *Sabbath as Resistance: Saying No to the Culture of Now* (Louisville, KY: Westminster John Knox, 2014), 11-12.

156 *serves as a framework for freedom*: Northumbria Community, "What is a Rule of Life?," accessed July 15, 2019, northumbriacommunity.org/who-we-are/our-rule-of-life/what-is-a-rule-of-life/.

157 *What would give [you]*: Allender, *Sabbath*, 113.

14. LIVING IN JOY

160 *I remember reading* The Prophet: Kahlil Gibran, *The Prophet* (New York: Alfred A. Knopf, 1923, 2001), 29.

162 *For anyone who has*: Henri Nouwen, *Can You Drink the Cup?* (Notre Dame, IN: Ave Maria Press, 1996), 46-47.

We need to be: Nouwen, *Can You Drink,* 74.

Suffering is inevitable: Dalai Lama XIV and Desmond Tutu, with Douglas Abrams, *The Book of Joy: Lasting Happiness in A Changing World* (New York: Avery Penguin Random House, 2016), 7, 11.

The more we turn toward: Lama XIV and Tutu, *The Book of Joy,* 62.

164 *For St. Ignatius, gratitude*: Kevin O'Brien, *The Ignatian Adventure: Experiencing the Ignatian Spiritual Exercises in Everyday Life* (Chicago: Loyola Press, 2011), 76.

Gratitude opens the heart: Dan B. Allender, *Sabbath* (Nashville, TN: Thomas Nelson, 2009), 140.

It is a daring act: Nouwen, *Can You Drink,* 75.

166 *"awe-and-wonder" walks*: Christine Aroney-Sine, *The Gift of Wonder: Creative Practices for Delighting in God* (Downers Grove, IL: InterVarsity Press, 2019), 32.

Humor creates a domino effect: Zelana Montminy, *21 Days to Resilience: How to Transcend the Daily Grind, Deal with the Tough Stuff, and Discover Your Strongest Stuff* (New York: HarperOne, 2016), 56.

We collectively need the release: Serene Jones, *Trauma and Grace: Theology in a Ruptured World* (Louisville, KY: Westminster John Knox, 2009), 35.

167 *benefits include a good mood*: "5 Benefits of Laughter Yoga," Laughter Yoga University, accessed April 24, 2020, laughteryoga.org/laughter-yoga/about-laughter-yoga/.

He says improv games: David Westerlund, "Improv for Nonprofits Caring for the Marginalized," presentation handout, September 13, 2018.

When we feel safe enough: David Westerlund, "Why I Do This Work," Be Present Discovery Joy, accessed September 13, 2018, bepresentdiscoverjoy.com.

169 *Laughter Yoga*: "Laughter Yoga in a Yoga Class, at Ashoka Park, New Delhi," YouTube, April 24, 2015, www.youtube.com/watch?v=1pScaHbverg.

Archbishop Desmond Tutu: "Archbishop Desmond Tutu Laughing—Leadership Live 2014," YouTube, May 7, 2015, www.youtube.com/watch?v=m66hwxypv8w.

CONCLUSION

171 *As I sat on a rock*: Lorie Martin, *Invited: Simple Prayer Exercises for Solitude and Community* (Abbotsford, BC: Fresh Wind Press, 2010), 27-29.

APPENDIX ONE: GROUNDING PRACTICES

179 *Begin by spending time*: Ruth Haley Barton, *Sacred Rhythms: Arranging Our Lives for Spiritual Transformation* (Downers Grove, IL: InterVarsity Press, 2006), 76.

APPENDIX TWO: REFLECTION AND PRAYER EXERCISES

184 *Based on Burden Bearing Prayer*: Lorie Martin, *Invited: Simple Prayer Exercises for Solitude and Community* (Abbotsford, BC: Fresh Wind Press, 2010), 203.

186 *The owner of the property*: Henry Cloud and John Townsend, *Boundaries: When to Say Yes and How to Say No to Take Control of Your Life* (Grand Rapids, MI: Zondervan, 2017), 30.

Based on Ruth Haley Barton's: Ruth Haley Barton, *Sacred Rhythms: Arranging Our Lives for Spiritual Transformation* (Downers Grove, IL: InterVarsity Press, 2006), 162.

Cheryl Richardson's The Art: Cheryl Richardson, *The Art of Extreme Self-Care: Transform Your Life One Month at a Time* (Carlsbad, CA: Hay House, 2009), 102-103.

Acknowledge the mystery: Barton, *Sacred Rhythms*, 163.

187 *Consider this exhortation from*: Barton, *Sacred Rhythms*, 145.